My Spiritual, Personal, Financial Journey Book

A Book of Daily Choices

By

Billie D. Hanes

authorHOUSE®

AuthorHouse™
1663 Liberty Drive
Bloomington, IN 47403
www.authorhouse.com
Phone: 1-800-839-8640

First published by AuthorHouse 1/25/2011

ISBN: 978-1-4567-3768-9 (e)
ISBN: 978-1-4567-3769-6 (sc)

Library of Congress Control Number: 2011901422

Printed in the United States of America

Any people depicted in stock imagery provided by Thinkstock are models,
and such images are being used for illustrative purposes only.
Certain stock imagery © Thinkstock.

This book is printed on acid-free paper.

Scripture quotations are taken from the Amplified Version of the Bible unless otherwise noted.

In Loving Memory

Billie Robena Parks Douglas, Mother

Patricia Ann Parks Smith, Sister

Table of Contents

Foreword

To my loving wife,

I dedicate these words of affection to express how much I love you and how proud I am of you. You have worked very hard to get where you are today and to complete this journey which you began in 2009 by keeping your faith in God and never letting go of His hand. I am so proud to be the husband of a strong and creative and helpful woman like you. This last year, you have proven that you are the woman that God has called you to be. With our girls, Ronetta, Janae, Erica, Janice, and Lavasia giving you inspiration along the way, I know this book will help others and exceed all expectations. Even with our grandchildren, Josiah and Zamiyah running through the house, you never took your eyes off the prize. We all love you and thank God each and every day for you. Many will be blessed because you completed the journey assigned to you.

-Bishop Franklin O. Hanes

Acknowledgements

What a journey this workbook has been for me. It grew out of the inspiration and desire to provide help for those who seemed to struggle with everyday life challenges, knowing the Word of God but not understanding how to apply the Word in certain areas of their lives, never seeming to get ahead. And even so, it is also for those who may have obtained a measure of success but know in their hearts that there is more, but may be lacking in the understanding of how to make "more" happen. There is a "good success" for those who are willing to meditate in God's Word and do the Word. That is what I pray this journey provides for anyone and everyone who will take it...an opportunity to have "good success" in their spiritual, personal and financial life.

First I give all the glory to God the Father, God the Son, and to God the Holy Spirit, without whom, this journey would not have been possible. I am grateful to my husband and pastor, Bishop Franklin O. Hanes who encourages and motivates me in my walk with Christ. I want to thank my girls, Ronetta, Janae, Janice, Erica and Lavasia, who are such an inspiration to me in their tenacity and boldness in service to the King. I also want to give a shout-out to my 'live-in' grand kids, Josiah and Zaymiah who kept me laughing, full of joy and busy throughout my journey. To my church family, The Greater Canaan Missionary Baptist Church, Mebane, NC, thank you for being there and for your constant support and prayers. You know I love you. And to the Douglas Family, you've always been there and I thank-you. Mavis, your insight and feedback have proven to be invaluable. And to the many other family and friends who've supported and encouraged me throughout this project, you are so appreciated.

A special "thanks" is also extended to Patrice Parrish and Deloris Gee. Your professional expertise and technical editing has ensured that a quality work is presented.

It's impossible for me to name everyone who has encouraged, inspired, motivated and helped me one way or another. I appreciate all of you and I am grateful that God has allowed our paths to cross and intermingle. Thank you, thank you, thank you.

-Rev. Billie D. Hanes

Introduction

This workbook is designed to assist you in making positive adjustments in your spiritual, personal, and financial thought life through decisions and choices based on the Word of God. As you make adjustments in your thoughts and speech, there will be manifested harvests from those adjustments in the natural over a period of time. You will only see the benefits of this book (the journey) if you choose to take the journey as outlined in the subsequent pages. No one can take this journey for you. No one can change your mind for your or make choices or speak for you. These are the necessary parts of the journey that you must choose to make for yourself. However, once you choose to take the journey, the Holy Spirit who is the Spirit of Truth, the Paraclete, the One who goes along beside, will be your constant companion providing the help that you need along the way.

The Journey Starts Now

You have a decision to make. If you're ready for positive changes in your spiritual, personal and financial life, if you're ready for positive changes in your spirit, soul and body, then you're ready for the journey. If you have chosen to take this journey and make positive adjustments in your thought life and what you say about yourself spiritually, financially and personally, take the time to read, fill in the blanks, sign, and date the statement below and get ready for positive change based on the promises of God's Word:

I, _____, on this the _____ day in the year of our Lord _____ do agree to begin and complete the journey as defined on the following pages of this book. I understand that the journey takes commitment and time, energy and effort, determination and consistency. I also understand that on this journey, there will be tests, trials, stumbling blocks, people, places, and things that seek to hinder me on the way and derail me from completing what I've chosen to begin. However, today and every day I choose to press on through anything and everything through the Truth of God's Word, for I know that there is a new, different, and better way of thinking and living at the end of this journey. I confess now that I can do all that I need to do through Christ who strengthens me to complete this journey.

(Signed) _____

Please allow me to pray for you as you begin this journey...

Father, I pray for my fellow laborer who has made the choice to take this spiritual, personal, and financial journey. I'm grateful for them and I ask you to bless them immeasurably along the way with the presence of Your Holy Spirit. Give them the desire, stamina, courage, and confidence needed to take this journey one day at a time. Help them to know and understand and believe without a shadow of doubt that they are able to do this through your beloved Son, Jesus Christ, in whose name I pray. Amen.

Welcome to "Your" Journey

Congratulations! You've actually taken the first step of the journey. You've made the choice to change or let's say, adjust positively the way you think and speak about your spiritual life, your personal life, and your financial life. Each of these areas is important, not just to you, but to God also. Planning to do something is a plan not to fail. By signing and dating the previous statement, you've chosen to do something about where you are now. You've recognized that faith without works is dead and you're putting your faith to work. You recognize that the valleys in your life can be exalted, every mountain made low and the crooked places made straight. You recognize that light will dispel darkness and bring about needed changes. Things will be different. Things will be better.

Every day is a good day to do something that you haven't done before, to explore new options, to make different choices, better choices. Every day is another opportunity to do the Word of God and not just hear the Word of God, for it is the doer of God's Word that will be endued with the power for success, prosperity, and longevity and will be given a rich and abundant life. Remember, you didn't get where you are overnight, so don't expect for everything around you or about you to change overnight. Expect things to get better. Expect increase!

Follow through with your commitment to yourself. Complete what you've started. Remember you are not alone.

Ready? Let's continue...

A word of precaution and encouragement....

In order to secure good results, it will be necessary for you to actively participate by completing the reading and writing assignments that are presented to you in this workbook. Don't give up before you even get started. You can do this! The flesh becomes very uncomfortable when asked to do what it is not accustomed to doing. Your flesh will not like anything about this workbook. You must be a doer of this work and not just a hearer. You must "keep under your body and bring it into subjection to your spirit". Your spirit is becoming attuned to God, your soul is becoming attuned to your spirit, and your body (flesh) hates it. Don't be embarrassed by your circumstances no matter what they are. Your circumstances are on the mend. Your situations are about to change, for the better. By making the choice to take this journey, you are placing all of your circumstances in God's hands. Rest assured. He is well able to handle them, no matter how big they seem, no matter how small they are and no matter how long they've been around. Wouldn't you agree? The point of being embarrassed or prideful and uncomfortable about the initial steps of your journey is what the enemy will try to use to hold you back or make you quit. Don't do what the enemy wants or expects you to do. Just hold on to this truth - this is the time to experience days of heaven – on earth!

Journey:

The daily choices and decisions made by an individual based on God's Word that allows them to leave one place of thought in order to arrive at another place of thought resulting in the manifestation of positive change while embracing the experiences along the way.

Me...

Since this is *your journey*, jot down a few things about yourself, why you've chosen to take this journey and what you hope to gain as a result.

A few things about me:

_____

_____

_____

_____

I have chosen to take this journey because:

_____

_____

_____

_____

_____

_____

Preparation...

Adequate preparation is a key factor in a successful journey. Make yourself ready for the journey by taking a look at where you are now and by thinking seriously about where you'd like to be a month, six months, and even a year from now. It's important to know where you're going; otherwise you may keep traveling around the same old tree, day after day after day, month after month after month, year after year after year, with no expectations and no results. Who among us doesn't have dreams or goals or desires? Maybe fear has held your dreams hostage and forbidden you to openly express them. Maybe lack has been that stumbling block that has prevented you from believing in your own dream or yourself. Maybe things that have been said to you in the past caused you to doubt and lose confidence in what you've held dear to your heart for so long. Well it's time for your dreams to be free. It's time to let go and let the God in You redeem what the 'maybes' tried to steal from you. Don't keep your dreams hidden in the back of your mind any longer. Let them out of that closet. If you keep your dreams in the back of your mind and never do anything about them, then why have a dream at all? You're responsible for your dream, for your vision, for your future. You must decide if your dream is worth having. And if it is, then you must map out a strategy to see to it that your dream comes to pass.

Here's your opportunity to do something about your dreams.

Write them down. This will be your goal, the desired result of taking the journey. Think about them, then, take a moment, no, take the necessary time to write them down. After all, *your* goals and dreams are important. Writing them is a great start to making your dreams come to pass. Habakkuk 2:2 reads *"And the Lord answered me and said, Write the vision and engrave it so plainly upon tablets that everyone who passes may [be able to] read [it easily and quickly] as he hastens by."* He's speaking to you right now. When you know where you're going, you're half-way there. Making the vision, your dreams, your goals, plain by writing them down will give you purpose for each day. By writing what's in your heart, you begin to breathe life into that dream; you cause it to come alive. Write what God has placed in your heart. He will give you the plans to make them happen, but remember, you must execute the plan. Just make sure that your goal is attainable. You may have a long-term goal, but there will be intermediate goals to get you there.

You've been given an entire page to write your vision. No fancy wording needed. You just need to clearly state your goal for the next year and you're the one who needs to understand what you've written. Maybe you can sum up your goals in a paragraph, or maybe a list will work best for you. Your goals should be meaningful and obtainable. Even though the sky is the limit when it comes to God, don't get out there too fast. Take your time. It's never too late. Your vision statement should include spiritual, personal, and financial goals. Okay, release that dream (vision, goals) from the closet of your mind; now start writing.

6

Goal:

God

Ordained

Abundant

Living

…

The desired end result achieved from the daily choices that one makes based on God's Word.

My Spiritual, Personal, and Financial Goals

(My Dream, Vision)

Spiritual:

_____

_____

_____

_____

Personal:

_____

_____

_____

_____

Financial:

_____

_____

_____

_____

Assistance...

Included in this workbook are weekly meditations, an annual goal sheet, monthly goals sheets, monthly tasks lists and appointments, monthly prayer requests and answers, a monthly budget worksheet, and celebration sheets.

The **annual goal sheet** is provided as a tool for you to discuss with family members goals for the entire family. It may be something as simple as painting the house, planting a garden, purchasing a new appliance, planning a monthly or bi-weekly family night out, increase giving to the church or a family vacation. Whatever your family goals may be, it is the opportunity for the family to work together towards common goals and ideas that you value as a family. These are not individual or personal goals, but these are goals that are family-based, goals for the entire household. Write them all down and then give each goal a priority. If the family vacation is the highest priority, it will be priority #1 and resources and plans should be allocated towards making that goal happen. Then set priority #2 and so on and so on. Set as many or as few as your family chooses to.

Use the **weekly meditations** to renew the spirit of your mind relative to your spiritual, personal, and financial life. It will be important for you to meditate on each scripture. Even though the meditations are given weekly, you should meditate on them every day, morning, noon, and at night. To meditate is to mutter, to rehearse over and over and over again. Read them aloud every day during the week (*faith comes by hearing and hearing by the word of God ... Romans 10:17*) and allow them to become a part of your thought life. Allow the Holy Spirit to give you understanding concerning the scripture. Then allow that scripture to become a part of your life by choosing to make daily decisions based on the scripture. Don't worry; the Holy Spirit will bring the scriptures to your remembrance as you plant them deep in your mind and heart through daily meditation. If you have a personal favorite scripture, one that speaks to your heart, by all means, make that a part of your weekly meditations in addition to the ones I've provided in the workbook.

The **monthly goal sheets** should be in agreement with the overall goals you set for yourself at the beginning of the workbook. These are reasonable, obtainable goals that you can achieve on a monthly basis that aid you in achieving your overall spiritual, personal, and financial goals. Step by step, you can make this journey and be successful. Remember, if you don't make any plans, then you've already planned to fail. Think about your overall goals and what you can do to work towards those goals within the current month. When you've finished thinking about them, write them down. You can do it!

Use the **monthly tasks lists** to identify the individual tasks needed to accomplish your monthly goals. For instance, if you have a monthly goal to lose five pounds, your task list may include to list the items you eat for a day. Then you may need to identify at least one item you can remove from your weekly diet that may be adding on some extra pounds or preventing you from losing pounds. Or maybe you want to save $10 this month (this is good if you haven't saved anything, it's a beginning). If you purchase lunch 3 to 4 times a week, bringing lunch an additional day or maybe even fasting at least 1 lunch a week may be a task to help you achieve the goal of saving $10 for the month. Whatever the task, make sure that it does not make you dependent upon someone else before it can happen. You are in control of your future. You and the Word of God decide what you can do, no one else. Use this sheet also to record any appointments that you may have for the month.

Prayer should be a part of your daily life. You should simply talk to God about what's in your heart and allow Him to talk to you about what's in His heart. You can tell Him absolutely anything and absolutely everything. However, don't allow your prayers to only be problem-centered. Pray the Word of God...pray the answer...and see it come to pass. Use the sheets provided to keep a record of your **prayer requests and also the answers** to those prayers. Make your request(s) and identify any scripture(s) that support your request(s). (This may require some research...a Bible concordance is a great tool for word searches.) Ensure that you're walking in obedience to God's Word concerning the request. Remember to keep praying...don't give up on the promises of GOD! Don't give up on your goals. This is definitely a faith builder. If He did it once, He'll do it again. If He did it for someone else, He can and will do it for you. If it doesn't happen this month, keep praying and keep believing. *Please consider the unsaved in your prayer time.* When recording the answers to your prayers, identify briefly the prayers you've prayed that have been answered. Show how the prayer has been answered and indicate the date you received the answer to your prayer. Remember to pray prayers of praise and thanksgiving. **GIVE GOD THANKS!**

A **monthly budget sheet**, who me? Yes you. You should be able to give an account of the monies that come into your hands. Waste not, want not. How will you ever grow financially if you don't know where you are financially? I'm sure you want to grow financially. This will mean doing what you haven't done before, or doing it better and doing it consistently. Keeping a budget will put you in control of your money and will keep your money or seemingly the lack thereof from controlling you. As you corral your finances, it will be challenging. But this is a necessary part of your financial journey. This is a necessary part of your financial growth. Use these budget sheets to track your financial journey. Work towards meeting your obligations on time and even before time. Thank God in your prayer time for financial wisdom. Thank God for enabling you to become a good steward over everything that He blesses you with. Prioritize your commitments. Put God first by giving tithes and offerings cheerfully for the advancement of God's kingdom, always...no matter what. Be a financial blessing to your Pastor(s). This may mean some sacrifices along the way. Maybe you can't eat out 5 days a week. You may need to limit yourself to 1 meal out during the week. Upon completing your spiritual 'financial' commitments of tithes and offerings, take care of your household items such as mortgage or rent, utilities and the like. Limit credit card usage or maybe strongly consider not using credit at all. The goal should be to get out of debt, not create more debt. Use layaway plans when possible or pay cash. Maybe you'll need to wait a while before making a purchase. Any sacrifice will be worth it as you work towards achieving the financial goals you've set for yourself. Be encouraged!

Now you deserve to **celebrate**! After you've established monthly goals, meditated in the Word of God, completed your tasks, prayed, tracked your finances, you deserve to celebrate. Use the **celebration sheets** to record how you rejoiced having accomplished your monthly commitments. Your celebration doesn't have to be extraordinarily big; it doesn't need to break the budget, but you need to reward yourself for following through with your commitment and completing your journey for the month. Once you complete the end of the workbook, pull out the fatted calf and really celebrate! You deserve it! Oh, if you missed the mark along the way, don't be hard on yourself. Thank God for the Blood of Jesus. Just get back up, shake off the dust and dirt, and keep traveling on your journey toward your goals.

There'll be a few surprises along the way, nothing to hurt you, only to encourage you and maybe even challenge you. I'm proud of you already. I am uplifted already about this. Aren't you? Okay, here you go... let the journey begin.

2011

JANUARY
Mo	Tu	We	Th	Fr	Sa	Su
31					1	2
3	4	5	6	7	8	9
10	11	12	13	14	15	16
17	18	19	20	21	22	23
24	25	26	27	28	29	30

FEBRUARY
Mo	Tu	We	Th	Fr	Sa	Su
	1	2	3	4	5	6
7	8	9	10	11	12	13
14	15	16	17	18	19	20
21	22	23	24	25	26	27
28						

MARCH
Mo	Tu	We	Th	Fr	Sa	Su
	1	2	3	4	5	6
7	8	9	10	11	12	13
14	15	16	17	18	19	20
21	22	23	24	25	26	27
28	29	30	31			

APRIL
Mo	Tu	We	Th	Fr	Sa	Su
				1	2	3
4	5	6	7	8	9	10
11	12	13	14	15	16	17
18	19	20	21	22	23	24
25	26	27	28	29	30	

MAY
Mo	Tu	We	Th	Fr	Sa	Su
30	31					1
2	3	4	5	6	7	8
9	10	11	12	13	14	15
16	17	18	19	20	21	22
23	24	25	26	27	28	29

JUNE
Mo	Tu	We	Th	Fr	Sa	Su
		1	2	3	4	5
6	7	8	9	10	11	12
13	14	15	16	17	18	19
20	21	22	23	24	25	26
27	28	29	30			

JULY
Mo	Tu	We	Th	Fr	Sa	Su
				1	2	3
4	5	6	7	8	9	10
11	12	13	14	15	16	17
18	19	20	21	22	23	24
25	26	27	28	29	30	31

AUGUST
Mo	Tu	We	Th	Fr	Sa	Su
1	2	3	4	5	6	7
8	9	10	11	12	13	14
15	16	17	18	19	20	21
22	23	24	25	26	27	28
29	30	31				

SEPTEMBER
Mo	Tu	We	Th	Fr	Sa	Su
			1	2	3	4
5	6	7	8	9	10	11
12	13	14	15	16	17	18
19	20	21	22	23	24	25
26	27	28	29	30		

OCTOBER
Mo	Tu	We	Th	Fr	Sa	Su
31					1	2
3	4	5	6	7	8	9
10	11	12	13	14	15	16
17	18	19	20	21	22	23
24	25	26	27	28	29	30

NOVEMBER
Mo	Tu	We	Th	Fr	Sa	Su
	1	2	3	4	5	6
7	8	9	10	11	12	13
14	15	16	17	18	19	20
21	22	23	24	25	26	27
28	29	30				

DECEMBER
Mo	Tu	We	Th	Fr	Sa	Su
			1	2	3	4
5	6	7	8	9	10	11
12	13	14	15	16	17	18
19	20	21	22	23	24	25
26	27	28	29	30	31	

2011

2012

JANUARY
Mo	Tu	We	Th	Fr	Sa	Su
30	31					1
2	3	4	5	6	7	8
9	10	11	12	13	14	15
16	17	18	19	20	21	22
23	24	25	26	27	28	29

FEBRUARY
Mo	Tu	We	Th	Fr	Sa	Su
		1	2	3	4	5
6	7	8	9	10	11	12
13	14	15	16	17	18	19
20	21	22	23	24	25	26
27	28	29				

MARCH
Mo	Tu	We	Th	Fr	Sa	Su
			1	2	3	4
5	6	7	8	9	10	11
12	13	14	15	16	17	18
19	20	21	22	23	24	25
26	27	28	29	30	31	

APRIL
Mo	Tu	We	Th	Fr	Sa	Su
30						1
2	3	4	5	6	7	8
9	10	11	12	13	14	15
16	17	18	19	20	21	22
23	24	25	26	27	28	29

MAY
Mo	Tu	We	Th	Fr	Sa	Su
	1	2	3	4	5	6
7	8	9	10	11	12	13
14	15	16	17	18	19	20
21	22	23	24	25	26	27
28	29	30	31			

JUNE
Mo	Tu	We	Th	Fr	Sa	Su
				1	2	3
4	5	6	7	8	9	10
11	12	13	14	15	16	17
18	19	20	21	22	23	24
25	26	27	28	29	30	

JULY
Mo	Tu	We	Th	Fr	Sa	Su
30	31					1
2	3	4	5	6	7	8
9	10	11	12	13	14	15
16	17	18	19	20	21	22
23	24	25	26	27	28	29

AUGUST
Mo	Tu	We	Th	Fr	Sa	Su
		1	2	3	4	5
6	7	8	9	10	11	12
13	14	15	16	17	18	19
20	21	22	23	24	25	26
27	28	29	30	31		

SEPTEMBER
Mo	Tu	We	Th	Fr	Sa	Su
					1	2
3	4	5	6	7	8	9
10	11	12	13	14	15	16
17	18	19	20	21	22	23
24	25	26	27	28	29	30

OCTOBER
Mo	Tu	We	Th	Fr	Sa	Su
1	2	3	4	5	6	7
8	9	10	11	12	13	14
15	16	17	18	19	20	21
22	23	24	25	26	27	28
29	30	31				

NOVEMBER
Mo	Tu	We	Th	Fr	Sa	Su
			1	2	3	4
5	6	7	8	9	10	11
12	13	14	15	16	17	18
19	20	21	22	23	24	25
26	27	28	29	30		

DECEMBER
Mo	Tu	We	Th	Fr	Sa	Su
31					1	2
3	4	5	6	7	8	9
10	11	12	13	14	15	16
17	18	19	20	21	22	23
24	25	26	27	28	29	30

2012

Annual Goal Sheet

Have a "family meeting". Explain the purpose of the meeting. Ask each member to talk about the goals and desires they'd like to see come to pass for the family, such as taking a family vacation or designing a family game room. Though everyone's goals or dreams are important, it's possible that not all of the goals identified will make the list this year. After discussing the pros and cons as well as the feasibility of each goal, come to agreement about the family goals for the year and write them on this sheet. You can have as many or as few as you like. Remember these are not personal or individual goals, but these are goals identified by the family for the family. Pray before the meeting begins and be sure to pray about the goals. Write the goals and give each one a priority. Establish a plan together that will allow you and your family to achieve the goals. Also plan to "meet" with the family periodically throughout the year to review the goals that have been identified and agreed upon as well as the progress that has been made towards achieving the goals.

1	
2	
3	
4	
5	
6	
7	
8	
9	
10	

And I am convinced and sure of this very thing, that He Who began a good work in you will continue until the day of Jesus Christ [right up to the time of his return], developing [that good work] and perfecting and bringing it to full completion in you.

~*Philippians 1:6*

January

January 2011

Mon	Tues	Wed	Thurs	Fri	Sat	Sun
					1 New Year's Day	2
3	4	5	6	7	8	9
10	11	12	13	14	15	16
17 MLK Jr. Day	18	19	20	21	22	23
24	25	26	27	28	29	30
31						

My Prayer Requests

Luke 18:1 ALSO [Jesus] told them a parable to the effect that they ought always to pray and not to turn coward (faint, lose heart, and give up).

Philippians 4:6 Do not fret or have any anxiety about anything, but in every circumstance and in everything, by prayer and petition (definite requests), with thanksgiving, continue to make your wants known to God.

Request	Scripture

Request	Scripture

Request	Scripture

Request	Scripture

Monthly Goals

Goal 1 – Spiritual

_____

_____

_____

Goal 2 – Personal

_____

_____

_____

Goal 3 – Financial

_____

_____

_____

Meditations

Week Ending 1-8-2011

Joshua 1:8

This Book of the Law shall not depart out of your mouth, but you shall meditate on it day and night, that you may observe and do according to all that is written in it. For then you shall make your way prosperous, and then you shall deal wisely and have good success

Matthew 6:31-33

Therefore do not worry and be anxious, saying, What are we going to have to eat? Or, What are we going to have to drink? Or, What are we going to have to wear?

For the Gentiles (heathen) wish for and crave and diligently seek all these things, and your heavenly Father knows well that you need them all.

But seek (aim at and strive after) first of all His kingdom and His righteousness (His way of doing and being right), and then all these things taken together will be given you besides.

Week Ending 1-15-2011

Matthew 11: 28-30

Come to Me, all you who labor and are heavy-laden and overburdened, and I will cause you to rest. [I will ease and relieve and refresh your souls.]

Take My yoke upon you and learn of Me, for I am gentle (meek) and humble (lowly) in heart, and you will find rest (relief and ease and refreshment and recreation and blessed quiet) for your souls.

For My yoke is wholesome (useful, good--not harsh, hard, sharp, or pressing, but comfortable, gracious, and pleasant), and My burden is light and easy to be borne.

Week Ending 1-22-2011

Psalm 86:5

For You, O Lord, are good, and ready to forgive [our trespasses, sending them away, letting them go completely and forever]; and You are abundant in mercy and loving-kindness to all those who call upon You.

I Corinthians 1:8-9

And He will establish you to the end [keep you steadfast, give you strength, and guarantee your vindication; He will be your warrant against all accusation or indictment so that you will be] guiltless and irreproachable in the day of our Lord Jesus Christ (the Messiah).

God is faithful (reliable, trustworthy, and therefore ever true to His promise, and He can be depended on); by Him you were called into companionship and participation with His Son, Jesus Christ our Lord.

Week Ending 1-29-2011

Romans 12:1-2

I appeal to you therefore, brethren, and beg of you in view of [all] the mercies of God, to make a decisive dedication of your bodies [presenting all your members and faculties] as a living sacrifice, holy (devoted, consecrated) and well pleasing to God, which is your reasonable (rational, intelligent) service and spiritual worship.

Do not be conformed to this world (this age), [fashioned after and adapted to its external, superficial customs], but be transformed (changed) by the [entire] renewal of your mind [by its new ideals and its new attitude], so that you may prove [for yourselves] what is the good and acceptable and perfect will of God, even the thing which is good and acceptable and perfect [in His sight for you].

I Corinthians 15:58

Therefore, my beloved brethren, be firm (**steadfast**), immovable, always abounding in the work of the Lord [always being superior, excelling, doing more than enough in the service of the Lord], knowing and being continually aware that your labor in the Lord is not futile [it is never wasted or to no purpose].

Monthly Tasks – Appointments

Task	✓
1	
2	
3	
4	
5	
6	
7	
8	

Appointment	Date/Time
1	
2	
3	
4	
5	
6	
7	
8	

Financial Meditation and Confession

Deuteronomy 15:4-6

However, there should be no poor among you, for in the land the LORD your God is giving you to possess as your inheritance; he will richly bless you,

if only you fully obey the LORD your God and are careful to follow all these commands I am giving you today.

For the LORD your God will bless you as he has promised, and you will lend to many nations but will borrow from none. You will rule over many nations but none will rule over you.

Confession

I am who the Lord God says I am and I can and will possess what the Lord says I will possess. I choose to fully obey the Lord my God and to carefully follow the commands that He gives to me daily. Therefore, He richly blesses me and empowers me to possess my inheritance. I am not poor and there are no poor among my family. He will bless me as He has promised. I will lend to many nations but I will not borrow from any. I will rule over many nations but not one nation will rule over me.

Personal Budget Worksheet

Income				
	Estimated	**Actual**		
Primary Pay				
Other 1				
Other 2				
Total Income				
Expenses				
	Estimated	**Actual**	**Due Date**	**Paid**
Church and Charities				
Tithes				
Offering				
Other Charity 1				
Other Charity 2				
Other Charity 3				
Household Expenses				
Rent/Mortgage				
Electricity				
Gas				
Water				
Grocery				
Household Supplies				
Home Insurance				
Repairs				
Taxes				

Personal Budget Worksheet (continued)

Household Expenses (cont.)				
	Estimated	**Actual**	**Due Date**	**Paid**
Land Phone				
Cable/Dish				
Other				
Car Expenses				
Car Payment				
Car Insurance				
Gas				
Taxes				
Maintenance/Repairs				
Debts				
Creditor 1				
Creditor 2				
Creditor 3				
Creditor 4				
Other				
Medical Expenses				
Medical Insurance				
Life Insurance				
Prescription Med(s)				
Other				

Personal Budget Worksheet (continued)

Other Expenses				
	Estimated	Actual	Due Date	Paid
Savings				
Cell Phone				
Children: Extra-Curricular				
Eateries & Entertainment				
Personal Grooming				
Organization/Club Dues				
Clothing				
Dry Cleaning				
Miscellaneous				
Miscellaneous 1				
Miscellaneous2				
Miscellaneous 3				
Miscellaneous 4				
Total Expenses				

Answers to My Prayers

I John 5:14-15 And this is the confidence (the assurance, the privilege of boldness) which we have in Him: [we are sure] that if we ask anything (make any request) according to His will (in agreement with His own plan), He listens to and hears us.

And if (since) we [positively] know that He listens to us in whatever we ask, we also know [with settled and absolute knowledge] that we have [granted us as our present possessions] the requests made of Him.

Request	Answer	Date Answered

Request	Answer	Date Answered

Request	Answer	Date Answered

Request	Answer	Date Answered

Celebration!

What you've accomplished this month deserves a celebration. Reward yourself for remaining true to your commitment, for remaining true to you. Invite a few friends over or have dinner out. Maybe go to a movie or a play, send yourself some flowers, but do something to commemorate your accomplishments. Maybe you didn't do everything that you wanted to do; maybe you didn't complete all your tasks or meet all of your goals, but if you've done anything, it's a positive step along the journey and is worth a celebration. Don't break the bank, but do rejoice. Make a note of how you celebrated your accomplishments.

_____

_____

_____

_____

_____

February

February 2011

Mon	Tues	Wed	Thurs	Fri	Sat	Sun
	1	2 Groundhog's Day	3	4	5	6
7	8	9	10	11	12	13
14 Valentine's Day	15	16	17	18	19	20
21 President's Day	22	23	24	25	26	27
28						

My Prayer Requests

James 5:16 Confess to one another therefore your faults (your slips, your false steps, your offenses, your sins) and pray [also] for one another, that you may be healed and restored [to a spiritual tone of mind and heart]. The earnest (heartfelt, continued) prayer of a righteous man makes tremendous power available [dynamic in its working].

Request	**Scripture**

Request	**Scripture**

Request	**Scripture**

Request	**Scripture**

Monthly Goals

Goal 1 – Spiritual

_____

_____

_____

Goal 2 – Personal

_____

_____

_____

Goal 3 – Financial

_____

_____

_____

Meditations

Week Ending 2-5-2011

Psalm 23

THE LORD is my Shepherd [to feed, guide, and shield me], I shall not lack.

He makes me lie down in [fresh, tender] green pastures; He leads me beside the still and restful waters.

He refreshes and restores my life (my self); He leads me in the paths of righteousness [uprightness and right standing with Him–not for my earning it, but] for His name's sake.

Yes, though I walk through the [deep, sunless] valley of the shadow of death, I will fear or dread no evil, for You are with me; Your rod [to protect] and Your staff [to guide], they comfort me.

You prepare a table before me in the presence of my enemies. You anoint my head with oil; my [brimming] cup runs over.

Surely or only goodness, mercy, and unfailing love shall follow me all the days of my life, and through the length of my days the house of the Lord [and His presence] shall be my dwelling place.

Week Ending 2-12-2011

Deuteronomy 11:8-15

Therefore you shall keep all the commandments which I command you today, that you may be strong and go in and possess the land which you go across [the Jordan] to possess,

And that you may live long in the land which the Lord swore to your fathers to give to them and to their descendants, a land flowing with milk and honey.

For the land which you go in to possess is not like the land of Egypt, from which you came out, where you sowed your seed and watered it with your foot laboriously as in a garden of vegetables.

But the land which you enter to possess is a land of hills and valleys which drinks water of the rain of the heavens,

A land for which the Lord your God cares; the eyes of the Lord your God are always upon it from the beginning of the year to the end of the year.

And if you will diligently heed My commandments which I command you this day--to love the Lord your God and to serve Him with all your [mind and] heart and with your entire being--

I will give the rain for your land in its season, the early rain and the latter rain, that you may gather in your grain, your new wine, and your oil.

And I will give grass in your fields for your cattle, that you may eat and be full.

Week Ending 2-19-2011

Romans 10:17

So faith comes by hearing [what is told], and what is heard comes by the preaching [of the message that came from the lips] of Christ (the Messiah Himself).

Hebrews 11:1-6

NOW FAITH is the assurance (the confirmation, the title deed) of the things [we] hope for, being the proof of things [we] do not see and the conviction of their reality [faith perceiving as real fact what is not revealed to the senses].

For by [faith--trust and holy fervor born of faith] the men of old had divine testimony borne to them and obtained a good report.

By faith we understand that the worlds [during the successive ages] were framed (fashioned, put in order, and equipped for their intended purpose) by the word of God, so that what we see was not made out of things which are visible.

[Prompted, actuated] by faith Abel brought God a better and more acceptable sacrifice than Cain, because of which it was testified of him that he was righteous [that he was upright and in right standing with God], and God bore witness by accepting and acknowledging his gifts. And though he died, yet [through the incident] he is still speaking.

Because of faith Enoch was caught up and transferred to heaven, so that he did not have a glimpse of death; and he was not found, because God had translated him. For even before he was taken to heaven, he received testimony [still on record] that he had pleased and been satisfactory to God.

But without faith it is impossible to please and be satisfactory to Him. For whoever would come near to God must [necessarily] believe that God exists and that He is the rewarder of those who earnestly and diligently seek Him [out].

Week Ending 2-26-2011

II Chronicles 32:7-8

Be strong and courageous. Be not afraid or dismayed before the king of Assyria and all the horde that is with him, for there is Another with us greater than [all those] with him.

With him is an arm of flesh, but with us is the Lord our God to help us and to fight our battles. And the people relied on the words of Hezekiah king of Judah.

Monthly Tasks – Appointments

Task	✓
1 _____	_____
2 _____	_____
3 _____	_____
4 _____	_____
5 _____	_____
6 _____	_____
7 _____	_____
8 _____	_____

Appointment	Date/Time
1 _____	_____
2 _____	_____
3 _____	_____
4 _____	_____
5 _____	_____
6 _____	_____
7 _____	_____
8 _____	_____

Financial Meditation and Confession

Psalm 1:1-3

BLESSED (HAPPY, fortunate, prosperous, and enviable) is the man who walks and lives not in the counsel of the ungodly [following their advice, their plans and purposes], nor stands [submissive and inactive] in the path where sinners walk, nor sits down [to relax and rest] where the scornful [and the mockers] gather.

But his delight and desire are in the law of the Lord, and on His law (the precepts, the instructions, the teachings of God) he habitually meditates (ponders and studies) by day and by night.

And he shall be like a tree firmly planted [and tended] by the streams of water, ready to bring forth its fruit in its season; its leaf also shall not fade or wither; and everything he does shall prosper [and come to maturity].

Confession

I am who the Lord God says I am and I can and will possess what the Lord says I will possess. I am happy, fortunate, and to be envied because I do not take counsel from those who do not know God. But I choose to delight myself in the law of the Lord daily. I meditate in the Word of God daily. Therefore I am like that tree, rooted and grounded by flowing water. I will bring forth in my season. I will produce. I will grow. I will prosper not in some things, but in all things that I set my heart to do.

Personal Budget Worksheet

Income				
	Estimated	**Actual**		
Primary Pay				
Other 1				
Other 2				
Total Income				
Expenses				
	Estimated	**Actual**	**Due Date**	**Paid**
Church and Charities				
Tithes				
Offering				
Other Charity 1				
Other Charity 2				
Other Charity 3				
Household Expenses				
Rent/Mortgage				
Electricity				
Gas				
Water				
Grocery				
Household Supplies				
Home Insurance				
Repairs				
Taxes				

Personal Budget Worksheet (continued)

Household Expenses (cont.)				
	Estimated	**Actual**	**Due Date**	**Paid**
Land Phone				
Cable/Dish				
Other				
Car Expenses				
Car Payment				
Car Insurance				
Gas				
Taxes				
Maintenance/Repairs				
Debts				
Creditor 1				
Creditor 2				
Creditor 3				
Creditor 4				
Other				
Medical Expenses				
Medical Insurance				
Life Insurance				
Prescription Med(s)				
Other				

Personal Budget Worksheet (continued)

Other Expenses				
	Estimated	**Actual**	**Due Date**	**Paid**
Savings				
Cell Phone				
Children: Extra-Curricular				
Eateries & Entertainment				
Personal Grooming				
Organization/Club Dues				
Clothing				
Dry Cleaning				
Miscellaneous				
Miscellaneous 1				
Miscellaneous2				
Miscellaneous 3				
Miscellaneous 4				
Total Expenses				

Answers to My Prayers

I Peter 3:12 For the eyes of the Lord are over the righteous, and his ears are open unto their prayers: but the face of the Lord is against them that do evil.

Request	Answer	Date Answered

Request	Answer	Date Answered

Request	Answer	Date Answered

Request	Answer	Date Answered

Celebration!

You did it again! I knew that you could. I trust that you're convinced also! Now **you know** that you can do this. Congratulations! Kick back and relax and think about how you want to "pat yourself on the back". Whatever you decide to do be sure to give testimony of the great things that God is doing in you and through you. I love it!

_____

_____

_____

_____

_____

_____

_____

March

March 2011

Mon	Tues	Wed	Thurs	Fri	Sat	Sun
	1	2	3	4	5	6
7	8	9 Ash Wednesday	10	11	12	13
14	15	16	17 St. Patrick's Day	18	19	20
21	22	23	24	25	26	27
28	29	30	31			

My Prayer Requests

I Timothy 2:1-2 FIRST OF all, then, I admonish and urge that petitions, prayers, intercessions, and thanksgivings be offered on behalf of all men,

For kings and all who are in positions of authority or high responsibility, that [outwardly] we may pass a quiet and undisturbed life [and inwardly] a peaceable one in all godliness and reverence and seriousness in every way.

Request	Scripture

Request	Scripture

Request	Scripture

Request	Scripture

Monthly Goals

Goal 1 – Spiritual

_____

_____

_____

Goal 2 – Personal

_____

_____

_____

Goal 3 – Financial

_____

_____

_____

Meditations

Week Ending 3-5-2011

Philippians 3:12-14

Not that I have now attained [this ideal], or have already been made perfect, but I press on to lay hold of (grasp) and make my own, that for which Christ Jesus (the Messiah) has laid hold of me and made me His own.

I do not consider, brethren, that I have captured and made it my own [yet]; but one thing I do [it is my one aspiration]: forgetting what lies behind and straining forward to what lies ahead,

I press on toward the goal to win the [supreme and heavenly] prize to which God in Christ Jesus is calling us upward.

Philippians 4:13

I have strength for all things in Christ Who empowers me [I am ready for anything and equal to anything through Him Who infuses inner strength into me; I am self-sufficient in Christ's sufficiency].

Week Ending 3-12-2011

Micah 6:6-8

With what shall I come before the Lord and bow myself before God on high? Shall I come before Him with burnt offerings, with calves a year old?

Will the Lord be pleased with thousands of rams or with ten thousands of rivers of oil? Shall I give my firstborn for my transgression, the fruit of my body for the sin of my soul?

He has showed you, O man, what is good. And what does the Lord require of you but to do justly, and to love kindness and mercy, and to humble yourself and walk humbly with your God?

Week Ending 3-19-2011

Psalm 46

GOD IS our Refuge and Strength [mighty and impenetrable to temptation], a very present and well-proved help in trouble.

Therefore we will not fear, though the earth should change and though the mountains be shaken into the midst of the seas,

Though its waters roar and foam, though the mountains tremble at its swelling and tumult. Selah [pause, and calmly think of that]!

There is a river whose streams shall make glad the city of God, the holy place of the tabernacles of the Most High.

God is in the midst of her, she shall not be moved; God will help her right early [at the dawn of the morning].

The nations raged, the kingdoms tottered and were moved; He uttered His voice, the earth melted.

The Lord of hosts is with us; the God of Jacob is our Refuge (our Fortress and High Tower). Selah [pause, and calmly think of that]!

Come, behold the works of the Lord, Who has wrought desolations and wonders in the earth.

He makes wars to cease to the end of the earth; He breaks the bow into pieces and snaps the spear in two; He burns the chariots in the fire.

Let be and be still, and know (recognize and understand) that I am God. I will be exalted among the nations! I will be exalted in the earth!

The Lord of hosts is with us; the God of Jacob is our Refuge (our High Tower and Stronghold). Selah [pause, and calmly think of that]!

Week Ending 3-26-2011

Isaiah 51:3

For the Lord will comfort Zion; He will comfort all her waste places. And He will make her wilderness like Eden, and her desert like the garden of the Lord. Joy and gladness will be found in her, thanksgiving and the voice of song or instrument of praise.

John 14:1-3

DO NOT let your hearts be troubled (distressed, agitated). You believe in and adhere to and trust in and rely on God; believe in and adhere to and trust in and rely also on Me.

In My Father's house there are many dwelling places (homes). If it were not so, I would have told you; for I am going away to prepare a place for you.

And when (if) I go and make ready a place for you, I will come back again and will take you to Myself, that where I am you may be also.

Monthly Tasks – Appointments

	Task	✓
1		
2		
3		
4		
5		
6		
7		
8		

	Appointment	Date/Time
1		
2		
3		
4		
5		
6		
7		
8		

Financial Meditation and Confession

Proverbs 3:5-10

Lean on, trust in, and be confident in the Lord with all your heart and mind and do not rely on your own insight or understanding.

In all your ways know, recognize, and acknowledge Him, and He will direct and make straight and plain your paths.

Be not wise in your own eyes; reverently fear and worship the Lord and turn [entirely] away from evil.

It shall be health to your nerves and sinews, and marrow and moistening to your bones.

Honor the Lord with your capital and sufficiency [from righteous labors] and with the firstfruits of all your income;

So shall your storage places be filled with plenty, and your vats shall be overflowing with new wine.

Confession

I am who the Lord God says I am and I can and will possess what the Lord says I will possess. I am leaning on, trusting in and confident in the Lord with all of my heart, not on what I see, feel, or hear. I am acknowledging Him daily and He directs me as to what I should do in every situation. I am not wise in my own eyes, but I rely on the spiritual understanding that God gives to me through His Word, I follow His instructions. I choose to honor the Lord with all that I have including the firstfruits of all my income. Therefore my storage places are filled. I have more than enough.

Personal Budget Worksheet

Income				
	Estimated	**Actual**		
Primary Pay				
Other 1				
Other 2				
Total Income				
Expenses				
	Estimated	**Actual**	**Due Date**	**Paid**
Church and Charities				
Tithes				
Offering				
Other Charity 1				
Other Charity 2				
Other Charity 3				
Household Expenses				
Rent/Mortgage				
Electricity				
Gas				
Water				
Grocery				
Household Supplies				
Home Insurance				
Repairs				
Taxes				

Personal Budget Worksheet (continued)

Household Expenses (cont.)				
	Estimated	**Actual**	**Due Date**	**Paid**
Land Phone				
Cable/Dish				
Other				
Car Expenses				
Car Payment				
Car Insurance				
Gas				
Taxes				
Maintenance/Repairs				
Debts				
Creditor 1				
Creditor 2				
Creditor 3				
Creditor 4				
Other				
Medical Expenses				
Medical Insurance				
Life Insurance				
Prescription Med(s)				
Other				

Personal Budget Worksheet (continued)

Other Expenses				
	Estimated	**Actual**	**Due Date**	**Paid**
Savings				
Cell Phone				
Children: Extra-Curricular				
Eateries & Entertainment				
Personal Grooming				
Organization/Club Dues				
Clothing				
Dry Cleaning				
Miscellaneous				
Miscellaneous 1				
Miscellaneous2				
Miscellaneous 3				
Miscellaneous 4				
Total Expenses				

Answers to My Prayers

Isaiah 55:11 So shall my word be that goeth forth out of my mouth: it shall not return unto me void, but it shall accomplish that which I please, and it shall prosper in the thing whereto I sent it.

Request	Answer	Date Answered

Request	Answer	Date Answered

Request	Answer	Date Answered

Request	Answer	Date Answered

Celebration!

Look at you! You're about to get it together. You're well on your way to being disciplined and planning to succeed in life. You made it through another month. You deserve a reward for the labor you've put in to your "journey" thus far. You're about to breakthrough to something great! Before you know it, you will have done all that you set your heart to do. You've made great strides now take your bow and do something awesome! Remember, make a note of how you celebrated your accomplishments this month.

_____

_____

_____

_____

_____

A Word of Encouragement

"It's Working for Your Good"

Romans 8:28 *We are assured and know that [God being a partner in their labor] all things work together and are [fitting into a plan] for good to and for those who love God and are called according to [His] design and purpose.*

How is it possible that the many trials and troubles you face in life from day to day can work for your good? Having the Almighty God as your Father is the answer to this and to many other questions and doubts that may come your way along this journey.

God is:
- Loving
- Benevolent
- Faithful
- Your heavenly Father

The Devil is:
- Your Enemy
- Wicked
- Not greater than your heavenly Father

God is:
- Always there to give you peace and joy in the midst of life's storms
- Always there to straighten out the curve balls that are thrown at you from every side
- Has a plan for your life that will come to pass
- Watches over you like a lioness watches over her cubs
- Never sleeps when it comes to you

Remember, God and you are a winning combination. Your love for Him will cause you to trust Him no matter who, no matter what, and no matter when. So don't be concerned about the bumps and the potholes in the road. Don't be concerned about the sharp curbs and falling rocks. In the end, you and others will see that it worked for good. Be assured, your heavenly Father is looking out for you. He's always fearless when it comes to you. He's always ready, willing and able when it comes to you. Be convinced in your own heart today, that everything, no matter what the thing is, it's working for your good. When it's all said and done, you will land on your feet. You will come out on top. You will be the victor and not the victim.

Let's Pray...

Father, Thank you that everything that happens to me is working for my good. Thank you for being in charge of my life, for having the final say. In Jesus' name. Amen.

Take a moment...reflect, review and write some personal notes and thoughts about the journey thus far. Say whatever you want to say. Think back and remember why you chose to take this journey from the beginning. YOU determine your success. This may also be a great time to review your personal annual goals as well as gather your family together to review the family goals. If you feel the need to make adjustments, it's okay, go ahead and make those adjustments. Be prayerful. God is with you. You are victorious. Just keep on keepin' on!

April

April 2011

Mon	Tues	Wed	Thurs	Fri	Sat	Sun
				1	2	3
4	5	6	7	8	9	10
11	12	13	14	15	16	17 Palm Sunday
18	19	20	21	22 Good Friday	23	24 Easter
25	26	27	28	29	30	

My Prayer Requests

Ephesians 6:18 Pray at all times (on every occasion, in every season) in the Spirit, with all [manner of] prayer and entreaty. To that end keep alert and watch with strong purpose and perseverance, interceding in behalf of all the saints (God's consecrated people).

Request	Scripture

Request	Scripture

Request	Scripture

Request	Scripture

Monthly Goals

Goal 1 – Spiritual

_____

_____

_____

Goal 2 – Personal

_____

_____

_____

Goal 3 – Financial

_____

_____

_____

Meditations

Week Ending 4-2-2011

II Corinthians 12:9-10

But He said to me, My grace (My favor and loving-kindness and mercy) is enough for you [sufficient against any danger and enables you to bear the trouble manfully]; for My strength and power are made perfect (fulfilled and completed) and show themselves most effective in [your] weakness. Therefore, I will all the more gladly glory in my weaknesses and infirmities, that the strength and power of Christ (the Messiah) may rest (yes, may pitch a tent over and dwell) upon me!

So for the sake of Christ, I am well pleased and take pleasure in infirmities, insults, hardships, persecutions, perplexities and distresses; for when I am weak [in human strength], then am I [truly] strong (able, powerful in divine strength).

Week Ending 4-9-2011

II Corinthians 4:8-10, 15-18

We are hedged in (pressed) on every side [troubled and oppressed in every way], but not cramped or crushed; we suffer embarrassments and are perplexed and unable to find a way out, but not driven to despair;

We are pursued (persecuted and hard driven), but not deserted [to stand alone]; we are struck down to the ground, but never struck out and destroyed;

Always carrying about in the body the liability and exposure to the same putting to death that the Lord Jesus suffered, so that the [resurrection] life of Jesus also may be shown forth by and in our bodies.

For all [these] things are [taking place] for your sake, so that the more grace (divine favor and spiritual blessing) extends to more and more people and multiplies through the many, the more thanksgiving may increase [and redound] to the glory of God.

Therefore we do not become discouraged (utterly spiritless, exhausted, and wearied out through fear). Though our outer man is [progressively] decaying and wasting away, yet our inner self is being [progressively] renewed day after day.

For our light, momentary affliction (this slight distress of the passing hour) is ever more and more abundantly preparing and producing and achieving for us an everlasting weight of glory [beyond all measure, excessively surpassing all comparisons and all calculations, a vast and transcendent glory and blessedness never to cease!],

Since we consider and look not to the things that are seen but to the things that are unseen; for the things that are visible are temporal (brief and fleeting), but the things that are invisible are deathless and everlasting.

Week Ending 4-16-2011

Psalm 103:1-5

BLESS (AFFECTIONATELY, gratefully praise) the Lord, O my soul; and all that is [deepest] within me, bless His holy name!

Bless (affectionately, gratefully praise) the Lord, O my soul, and forget not [one of] all His benefits--

Who forgives [every one of] all your iniquities, Who heals [each one of] all your diseases,

Who redeems your life from the pit and corruption, Who beautifies, dignifies, and crowns you with loving-kindness and tender mercy;

Who satisfies your mouth [your necessity and desire at your personal age and situation] with good so that your youth, renewed, is like the eagle's [strong, overcoming, soaring]!

Week Ending 4-23-2011

John 3:16

For God so greatly loved and dearly prized the world that He [even] gave up His only begotten (unique) Son, so that whoever believes in (trusts in, clings to, relies on) Him shall not perish (come to destruction, be lost) but have eternal (everlasting) life.

I John 4:7-11

Beloved, let us love one another, for love is (springs) from God; and he who loves [his fellowmen] is begotten (born) of God and is coming [progressively] to know and understand God [to perceive and recognize and get a better and clearer knowledge of Him].

He who does not love has not become acquainted with God [does not and never did know Him], for God is love.

In this the love of God was made manifest (displayed) where we are concerned: in that God sent His Son, the only begotten or unique [Son], into the world so that we might live through Him.

In this is love: not that we loved God, but that He loved us and sent His Son to be the propitiation (the atoning sacrifice) for our sins.

Beloved, if God loved us so [very much], we also ought to love one another.

Week Ending 4-30-2011

Romans 8:35-39

Who shall ever separate us from Christ's love? Shall suffering and affliction and tribulation? Or calamity and distress? Or persecution or hunger or destitution or peril or sword?

Even as it is written, For Thy sake we are put to death all the day long; we are regarded and counted as sheep for the slaughter.

Yet amid all these things we are more than conquerors and gain a surpassing victory through Him Who loved us.

 For I am persuaded beyond doubt (am sure) that neither death nor life, nor angels nor principalities, nor things impending and threatening nor things to come, nor powers,

Nor height nor depth, nor anything else in all creation will be able to separate us from the love of God which is in Christ Jesus our Lord.

Monthly Tasks – Appointments

	Task	✓
1		
2		
3		
4		
5		
6		
7		
8		

	Appointment	Date/Time
1		
2		
3		
4		
5		
6		
7		
8		

Financial Meditation and Confession

Deuteronomy 15:4-6

However, there should be no poor among you, for in the land the LORD your God is giving you to possess as your inheritance, he will richly bless you,

if only you fully obey the LORD your God and are careful to follow all these commands I am giving you today.

For the LORD your God will bless you as he has promised, and you will lend to many nations but will borrow from none. You will rule over many nations but none will rule over you.

Confession

I am who the Lord God says I am and I can and will possess what the Lord says I will possess. I choose to fully obey the Lord my God and to carefully follow the commands that He gives to me daily. Therefore, He richly blesses me and empowers me to possess my inheritance. I am not poor and there are no poor among my family. He will bless me as He has promised. I will lend to many nations but I will not borrow from any. I will rule over many nations but not one nation will rule over me.

Personal Budget Worksheet

Income				
	Estimated	**Actual**		
Primary Pay				
Other 1				
Other 2				
Total Income				
Expenses				
	Estimated	**Actual**	**Due Date**	**Paid**
Church and Charities				
Tithes				
Offering				
Other Charity 1				
Other Charity 2				
Other Charity 3				
Household Expenses				
Rent/Mortgage				
Electricity				
Gas				
Water				
Grocery				
Household Supplies				
Home Insurance				
Repairs				
Taxes				

Personal Budget Worksheet (continued)

Household Expenses (cont.)				
	Estimated	**Actual**	**Due Date**	**Paid**
Land Phone				
Cable/Dish				
Other				
Car Expenses				
Car Payment				
Car Insurance				
Gas				
Taxes				
Maintenance/Repairs				
Debts				
Creditor 1				
Creditor 2				
Creditor 3				
Creditor 4				
Other				
Medical Expenses				
Medical Insurance				
Life Insurance				
Prescription Med(s)				
Other				

Personal Budget Worksheet (continued)

Other Expenses				
	Estimated	Actual	Due Date	Paid
Savings				
Cell Phone				
Children: Extra-Curricular				
Eateries & Entertainment				
Personal Grooming				
Organization/Club Dues				
Clothing				
Dry Cleaning				
Miscellaneous				
Miscellaneous 1				
Miscellaneous2				
Miscellaneous 3				
Miscellaneous 4				
Total Expenses				

Answers to My Prayers

I Samuel 30:8 And David enquired at the LORD, saying, Shall I pursue after this troop? shall I overtake them? And he answered him, Pursue: for thou shalt surely overtake them, and without fail recover all.

Request	Answer	Date Answered

Request	Answer	Date Answered

Request	Answer	Date Answered

Request	Answer	Date Answered

Celebration!

I believe that you're unstoppable. You've proven that the Word of God is true...It's possible when you believe it's possible. I know you thought you wouldn't make it this far, but you did. Hallelujah! You're taking the journey and the journey is working for you. Don't hold back. Rejoice in the Lord! Do something that you've always wanted to do, but never did (within reason, you're still on a budget) to commemorate the occasion. Remember to write down how you chose to celebrate this milestone on your journey.

_____

_____

_____

_____

_____

_____

May

May 2011

Mon	Tues	Wed	Thurs	Fri	Sat	Sun
						1
2	3	4	5	6	7	8 Mother's Day
9	10	11	12	13	14	15
16	17	18	19	20	21	22
23	24	25	26	27	28	29
30 Memorial Day	31					

My Prayer Requests

I Peter 5:6-7 Therefore humble yourselves [demote, lower yourselves in your own estimation] under the mighty hand of God, that in due time He may exalt you,

Casting the whole of your care [all your anxieties, all your worries, all your concerns, once and for all] on Him, for He cares for you affectionately and cares about you watchfully.

Request	Scripture
Request	**Scripture**
Request	**Scripture**
Request	**Scripture**

Monthly Goals

Goal 1 – Spiritual

_____

_____

_____

Goal 2 – Personal

_____

_____

_____

Goal 3 – Financial

_____

_____

_____

Meditations

Week Ending 5-7-2011

Mark 12:29-31

Jesus answered, The first and principal one of all commands is: Hear, O Israel, The Lord our God is one Lord;

And you shall love the Lord your God out of and with your whole heart and out of and with all your soul (your life) and out of and with all your mind (with your faculty of thought and your moral understanding) and out of and with all your strength. This is the first and principal commandment.

The second is like it and is this, You shall love your neighbor as yourself. There is no other commandment greater than these.

Week Ending 5-14-2011

Lamentations 3:22-26

It is because of the Lord's mercy and loving-kindness that we are not consumed, because His [tender] compassions fail not.

They are new every morning; great and abundant is Your stability and faithfulness.

The Lord is my portion or share, says my living being (my inner self); therefore will I hope in Him and wait expectantly for Him.

The Lord is good to those who wait hopefully and expectantly for Him, to those who seek Him [inquire of and for Him and require Him by right of necessity and on the authority of God's word].

It is good that one should hope in and wait quietly for the salvation (the safety and ease) of the Lord.

Week Ending 5-21-2011

Matthew 7:24-27

So everyone who hears these words of Mine and acts upon them [obeying them] will be like a sensible (prudent, practical, wise) man who built his house upon the rock.

And the rain fell and the floods came and the winds blew and beat against that house; yet it did not fall, because it had been founded on the rock.

And everyone who hears these words of Mine and does not do them will be like a stupid (foolish) man who built his house upon the sand.

And the rain fell and the floods came and the winds blew and beat against that house, and it fell--and great and complete was the fall of it.

Week Ending 5-28-2011

Colossians 3:1-9

IF THEN you have been raised with Christ [to a new life, thus sharing His resurrection from the dead], aim at and seek the [rich, eternal treasures] that are above, where Christ is, seated at the right hand of God.

And set your minds and keep them set on what is above (the higher things), not on the things that are on the earth.

For [as far as this world is concerned] you have died, and your [new, real] life is hidden with Christ in God.

When Christ, Who is our life, appears, then you also will appear with Him in [the splendor of His] glory.

So kill (deaden, deprive of power) the evil desire lurking in your members [those animal impulses and all that is earthly in you that is employed in sin]: sexual vice, impurity, sensual appetites, unholy desires, and all greed and covetousness, for that is idolatry (the deifying of self and other created things instead of God).

It is on account of these [very sins] that the [holy] anger of God is ever coming upon the sons of disobedience (those who are obstinately opposed to the divine will),

Among whom you also once walked, when you were living in and addicted to [such practices].

But now put away and rid yourselves [completely] of all these things: anger, rage, bad feeling toward others, curses and slander, and foulmouthed abuse and shameful utterances from your lips!

Do not lie to one another, for you have stripped off the old (unregenerate) self with its evil practices

Monthly Tasks – Appointments

Task	✓
1	
2	
3	
4	
5	
6	
7	
8	

Appointment	Date/Time
1	
2	
3	
4	
5	
6	
7	
8	

Financial Meditation and Confession

Luke 6:38

Give, and [gifts] will be given to you; good measure, pressed down, shaken together, and running over, will they pour into [the pouch formed by] the bosom [of your robe and used as a bag]. For with the measure you deal out [with the measure you use when you confer benefits on others], it will be measured back to you.

Confession

I am who the Lord God says I am and I can and will possess what the Lord says I will possess. I am a giver. My Father God is a giver and so am I. I choose to give liberally according to the Word of God, a measure that would be acceptable and pleasing in God's sight. And because I give, gifts are given to me; the measure is given back to me. But God takes that measure, presses it down, shakes it together such that it runs over. Hallelujah! I choose to be a blessing in the earth, to benefit others and that same blessing is bestowed upon me.

Personal Budget Worksheet

Income				
	Estimated	**Actual**		
Primary Pay				
Other 1				
Other 2				
Total Income				
Expenses				
	Estimated	**Actual**	**Due Date**	**Paid**
Church and Charities				
Tithes				
Offering				
Other Charity 1				
Other Charity 2				
Other Charity 3				
Household Expenses				
Rent/Mortgage				
Electricity				
Gas				
Water				
Grocery				
Household Supplies				
Home Insurance				
Repairs				
Taxes				

Personal Budget Worksheet (continued)

Household Expenses (cont.)				
	Estimated	Actual	Due Date	Paid
Land Phone				
Cable/Dish				
Other				
Car Expenses				
Car Payment				
Car Insurance				
Gas				
Taxes				
Maintenance/Repairs				
Debts				
Creditor 1				
Creditor 2				
Creditor 3				
Creditor 4				
Other				
Medical Expenses				
Medical Insurance				
Life Insurance				
Prescription Med(s)				
Other				

Personal Budget Worksheet (continued)

Other Expenses				
	Estimated	**Actual**	**Due Date**	**Paid**
Savings				
Cell Phone				
Children: Extra-Curricular				
Eateries & Entertainment				
Personal Grooming				
Organization/Club Dues				
Clothing				
Dry Cleaning				
Miscellaneous				
Miscellaneous 1				
Miscellaneous2				
Miscellaneous 3				
Miscellaneous 4				
Total Expenses				

Answers to My Prayers

John 16:23-24   And when that time comes, you will ask nothing of Me [you will need to ask Me no questions]. I assure you, most solemnly I tell you, that My Father will grant you whatever you ask in My Name [as presenting all that I AM].

Up to this time you have not asked a [single] thing in My Name [as presenting all that I AM]; but now ask and keep on asking and you will receive, so that your joy (gladness, delight) may be full and complete.

Request	Answer	Date Answered

Request	Answer	Date Answered

Request	Answer	Date Answered

Request	Answer	Date Answered

Celebration!

I have to congratulate you. You've kept the faith. You've persevered. I know that you may have been challenged, but you held on and didn't give up. In spite of any obstacles, any troubles or temptations, in spite of anything you've faced, you didn't quit and that deserves an honorable mention and a celebration! These are indeed good times. Now reward yourself. Maybe partner with someone you know who may also be taking this journey and celebrate together. Whatever you do, do something and record the celebration below! I'm so proud of you and you should be proud of yourself!

_____

_____

_____

_____

_____

_____

June

June 2011

Mon	Tues	Wed	Thurs	Fri	Sat	Sun
		1	2	3	4	5
6	7	8	9	10	11	12
13	14 Flag Day	15	16	17	18	19 Father's Day
20	21	22	23	24	25	26
27	28	29	30			

My Prayer Requests

Isaiah 43:25-26 I, even I, am He Who blots out and cancels your transgressions, for My own sake, and I will not remember your sins.

Put Me in remembrance [remind Me of your merits]; let us plead and argue together. Set forth your case, that you may be justified (proved right).

Request	**Scripture**

Request	**Scripture**

Request	**Scripture**

Request	**Scripture**

Monthly Goals

Goal 1 – Spiritual

_____

_____

_____

Goal 2 – Personal

_____

_____

_____

Goal 3 – Financial

_____

_____

_____

Meditations

Week Ending 6-4-2011

Deuteronomy 28: 1-14

IF YOU will listen diligently to the voice of the Lord your God, being watchful to do all His commandments which I command you this day, the Lord your God will set you high above all the nations of the earth.

And all these blessings shall come upon you and overtake you if you heed the voice of the Lord your God.

Blessed shall you be in the city and blessed shall you be in the field.

Blessed shall be the fruit of your body and the fruit of your ground and the fruit of your beasts, the increase of your cattle and the young of your flock.

Blessed shall be your basket and your kneading trough.

Blessed shall you be when you come in and blessed shall you be when you go out.

The Lord shall cause your enemies who rise up against you to be defeated before your face; they shall come out against you one way and flee before you seven ways.

The Lord shall command the blessing upon you in your storehouse and in all that you undertake. And He will bless you in the land which the Lord your God gives you.

The Lord will establish you as a people holy to Himself, as He has sworn to you, if you keep the commandments of the Lord your God and walk in His ways.

And all people of the earth shall see that you are called by the name [and in the presence of] the Lord, and they shall be afraid of you.

And the Lord shall make you have a surplus of prosperity, through the fruit of your body, of your livestock, and of your ground, in the land which the Lord swore to your fathers to give you.

The Lord shall open to you His good treasury, the heavens, to give the rain of your land in its season and to bless all the work of your hands; and you shall lend to many nations, but you shall not borrow.

And the Lord shall make you the head, and not the tail; and you shall be above only, and you shall not be beneath, if you heed the commandments of the Lord your God which I command you this day and are watchful to do them.

And you shall not turn aside from any of the words which I command you this day, to the right hand or to the left, to go after other gods to serve them.

Week Ending 6-11-2011

Psalm 91:1-7

HE WHO dwells in the secret place of the Most High shall remain stable and fixed under the shadow of the Almighty [Whose power no foe can withstand].

I will say of the Lord, He is my Refuge and my Fortress, my God; on Him I lean and rely, and in Him I [confidently] trust!

For [then] He will deliver you from the snare of the fowler and from the deadly pestilence.

[Then] He will cover you with His pinions, and under His wings shall you trust and find refuge; His truth and His faithfulness are a shield and a buckler.

You shall not be afraid of the terror of the night, nor of the arrow (the evil plots and slanders of the wicked) that flies by day,

Nor of the pestilence that stalks in darkness, nor of the destruction and sudden death that surprise and lay waste at noonday.

A thousand may fall at your side, and ten thousand at your right hand, but it shall not come near you.

Week Ending 6-18-2011

Ephesians 6:10-18

In conclusion, be strong in the Lord [be empowered through your union with Him]; draw your strength from Him [that strength which His boundless might provides].

Put on God's whole armor [the armor of a heavy-armed soldier which God supplies], that you may be able successfully to stand up against [all] the strategies and the deceits of the devil.

For we are not wrestling with flesh and blood [contending only with physical opponents], but against the despotisms, against the powers, against [the master spirits who are] the world rulers of this present darkness, against the spirit forces of wickedness in the heavenly (supernatural) sphere.

Therefore put on God's complete armor, that you may be able to resist and stand your ground on the evil day [of danger], and, having done all [the crisis demands], to stand [firmly in your place].

Stand therefore [hold your ground], having tightened the belt of truth around your loins and having put on the breastplate of integrity and of moral rectitude and right standing with God,

And having shod your feet in preparation [to face the enemy with the firm-footed stability, the promptness, and the readiness produced by the good news] of the Gospel of peace.

Lift up over all the [covering] shield of saving faith, upon which you can quench all the flaming missiles of the wicked [one].

And take the helmet of salvation and the sword that the Spirit wields, which is the Word of God.

Pray at all times (on every occasion, in every season) in the Spirit, with all [manner of] prayer and entreaty. To that end keep alert and watch with strong purpose and perseverance, interceding in behalf of all the saints (God's consecrated people).

Week Ending 6-25-2011

Proverbs 1:7

The reverent and worshipful fear of the Lord is the beginning and the principal and choice part of knowledge [its starting point and its essence]; but fools despise skillful and godly Wisdom, instruction, and discipline.

Proverbs 2:1-5

MY SON, if you will receive my words and treasure up my commandments within you,

Making your ear attentive to skillful and godly Wisdom and inclining and directing your heart and mind to understanding [applying all your powers to the quest for it];

Yes, if you cry out for insight and raise your voice for understanding,

If you seek [Wisdom] as for silver and search for skillful and godly Wisdom as for hidden treasures,

Then you will understand the reverent and worshipful fear of the Lord and find the knowledge of [our omniscient] God.

Monthly Tasks – Appointments

Task	✓
1	
2	
3	
4	
5	
6	
7	
8	

Appointment	Date/Time
1	
2	
3	
4	
5	
6	
7	
8	

Financial Meditation and Confession

Mark 10:29-31

Jesus said, Truly I tell you, there is no one who has given up and left house or brothers or sisters or mother or father or children or lands for My sake and for the Gospel's

Who will not receive a hundred times as much now in this time--houses and brothers and sisters and mothers and children and lands, with persecutions--and in the age to come, eternal life.

But many [who are now] first will be last [then], and many [who are now] last will be first [then].

Confession

I am who the Lord God says I am and I can and will possess what the Lord says I will possess. I choose to lose my life in order to gain His life and His abundance. I make the appropriate sacrifices and put no one and nothing before God and the Gospel. I am a recipient of the hundred fold blessings in houses, brothers, sisters, mothers, children and lands, both in this life and in the life to come. Though persecuted, God delivers me and empowers me to remain victorious. No longer am I last, but through the blessings of Almighty God, He makes me first. Hallelujah!

Personal Budget Worksheet

Income				
	Estimated	**Actual**		
Primary Pay				
Other 1				
Other 2				
Total Income				
Expenses				
	Estimated	**Actual**	**Due Date**	**Paid**
Church and Charities				
Tithes				
Offering				
Other Charity 1				
Other Charity 2				
Other Charity 3				
Household Expenses				
Rent/Mortgage				
Electricity				
Gas				
Water				
Grocery				
Household Supplies				
Home Insurance				
Repairs				
Taxes				

Personal Budget Worksheet (continued)

Household Expenses (cont.)				
	Estimated	Actual	Due Date	Paid
Land Phone				
Cable/Dish				
Other				
Car Expenses				
Car Payment				
Car Insurance				
Gas				
Taxes				
Maintenance/Repairs				
Debts				
Creditor 1				
Creditor 2				
Creditor 3				
Creditor 4				
Other				
Medical Expenses				
Medical Insurance				
Life Insurance				
Prescription Med(s)				
Other				

Personal Budget Worksheet (continued)

Other Expenses				
	Estimated	Actual	Due Date	Paid
Savings				
Cell Phone				
Children: Extra-Curricular				
Eateries & Entertainment				
Personal Grooming				
Organization/Club Dues				
Clothing				
Dry Cleaning				
Miscellaneous				
Miscellaneous 1				
Miscellaneous2				
Miscellaneous 3				
Miscellaneous 4				
Total Expenses				

Answers to My Prayers

Ephesians 3:20 Now to Him Who, by (in consequence of) the [action of His] power that is at work within us, is able to [carry out His purpose and] do superabundantly, far over and above all that we [dare] ask or think [infinitely beyond our highest prayers, desires, thoughts, hopes, or dreams].

Request	Answer	Date Answered

Request	Answer	Date Answered

Request	Answer	Date Answered

Request	Answer	Date Answered

Celebration!

You've completed your sixth month. You're closer this month than you were last month to completing the journey. You're well on your way to achieving the God Ordained Abundant Living that has been promised to you as a child of God. Remember, this is your journey, and you deserve to celebrate all accomplishments. Each completed tasks, no matter how big or small, brings you closer to achieving your goal. With that said, take in a movie, go see a play, spend some time fellowshipping with your friends. Just know that it's your time now to celebrate!

_____

_____

_____

_____

_____

July

July 2011

Mon	Tues	Wed	Thurs	Fri	Sat	Sun
				1	2	3
4 Independence Day	5	6	7	8	9	10
11	12	13	14	15	16	17
18	19	20	21	22	23	24
25	26	27	28	29	30	31

My Prayer Requests

Hebrews 4:14, 16 Inasmuch then as we have a great High Priest Who has [already] ascended and passed through the heavens, Jesus the Son of God, let us hold fast our confession [of faith in Him]. .... Let us then fearlessly and confidently and boldly draw near to the throne of grace (the throne of God's unmerited favor to us sinners), that we may receive mercy [for our failures] and find grace to help in good time for every need [appropriate help and well-timed help, coming just when we need it].

Request	Scripture

Request	Scripture

Request	Scripture

Request	Scripture

Monthly Goals

Goal 1 – Spiritual

_____

_____

_____

Goal 2 – Personal

_____

_____

_____

Goal 3 – Financial

_____

_____

_____

Meditations

Week Ending 7-2-2011

Exodus 15:1-3, 11

THEN MOSES and the Israelites sang this song to the Lord, saying, I will sing to the Lord, for He has triumphed gloriously; the horse and his rider or its chariot has He thrown into the sea.

The Lord is my Strength and my Song, and He has become my Salvation; this is my God, and I will praise Him, my father's God, and I will exalt Him.

The Lord is a Man of War; the Lord is His name.

Who is like You, O Lord, among the gods? Who is like You, glorious in holiness, awesome in splendor, doing wonders?

Week Ending 7-9-2011

I John 2:15-17

Do not love or cherish the world or the things that are in the world. If anyone loves the world, love for the Father is not in him.

For all that is in the world--the lust of the flesh [craving for sensual gratification] and the lust of the eyes [greedy longings of the mind] and the pride of life [assurance in one's own resources or in the stability of earthly things]--these do not come from the Father but are from the world [itself].

And the world passes away and disappears, and with it the forbidden cravings (the passionate desires, the lust) of it; but he who does the will of God and carries out His purposes in his life abides (remains) forever.

Week Ending 7-16-2011

Hebrews 11:1, 6

NOW FAITH is the assurance (the confirmation, the title deed) of the things [we] hope for, being the proof of things [we] do not see and the conviction of their reality [faith perceiving as real fact what is not revealed to the senses].

But without faith it is impossible to please and be satisfactory to Him. For whoever would come near to God must [necessarily] believe that God exists and that He is the rewarder of those who earnestly and diligently seek Him [out].

Week Ending 7-23-2011

I Chronicles 16:23-36

Sing to the Lord, all the earth; show forth from day to day His salvation.

Declare His glory among the nations, His marvelous works among all peoples.

For great is the Lord and greatly to be praised; He also is to be [reverently] feared above all so-called gods.

For all the gods of the people are [lifeless] idols, but the Lord made the heavens.

Honor and majesty are [found] in His presence; strength and joy are [found] in His sanctuary.

Ascribe to the Lord, you families of the peoples, ascribe to the Lord glory and strength,

Ascribe to the Lord the glory due His name. Bring an offering and come before Him; worship the Lord in the beauty of holiness and in holy array.

Tremble and reverently fear before Him, all the earth's peoples; the world also shall be established, so it cannot be moved.

Let the heavens be glad and let the earth rejoice; and let men say among the nations, The Lord reigns!

Let the sea roar, and all the things that fill it; let the fields rejoice, and all that is in them.

Then shall the trees of the wood sing out for joy before the Lord, for He comes to judge and govern the earth.

O give thanks to the Lord, for He is good; for His mercy and loving-kindness endure forever!

And say, Save us, O God of our salvation; gather us together and deliver us from the nations, that we may give thanks to Your holy name and glory in Your praise.

Blessed be the Lord, the God of Israel, forever and ever! And all the people said Amen! and praised the Lord.

Week Ending 7-23-2011

Luke 6:19-23

And all the multitude were seeking to touch Him, for healing power was all the while going forth from Him and curing them all [saving them from severe illnesses or calamities].

And solemnly lifting up His eyes on His disciples, He said: Blessed (happy--with life-joy and satisfaction in God's favor and salvation, apart from your outward condition--and to be envied) are you poor and lowly and afflicted (destitute of wealth, influence, position, and honor), for the kingdom of God is yours!

Blessed (happy--with life-joy and satisfaction in God's favor and salvation, apart from your outward condition--and to be envied) are you who hunger and seek with eager desire now, for you shall be filled and completely satisfied! Blessed (happy--with life-joy and satisfaction in God's favor and salvation, apart from your outward condition--and to be envied) are you who weep and sob now, for you shall laugh!

Blessed (happy--with life-joy and satisfaction in God's favor and salvation, apart from your outward condition--and to be envied) are you when people despise (hate) you, and when they exclude and excommunicate you [as disreputable] and revile and denounce you and defame and cast out and spurn your name as evil (wicked) on account of the Son of Man.

Rejoice and be glad at such a time and exult and leap for joy, for behold, your reward is rich and great and strong and intense and abundant in heaven; for even so their forefathers treated the prophets.

Monthly Tasks – Appointments

Task	✓
1	
2	
3	
4	
5	
6	
7	
8	

Appointment	Date/Time
1	
2	
3	
4	
5	
6	
7	
8	

Financial Meditation and Confession

Psalm 34:9-10

O fear the Lord, you His saints [revere and worship Him]! For there is no want to those who truly revere and worship Him with godly fear.

The young lions lack food and suffer hunger, but they who seek (inquire of and require) the Lord [by right of their need and on the authority of His Word], none of them shall lack any beneficial thing.

Confession

I am who the Lord God says I am and I can and will possess what the Lord says I will possess. I fear the Lord. I reverence the Lord. I honor and worship Him and Him only. I do not want for anything, not houses, clothes, land, food, money, happiness, peace, joy, love, no...I do not want for anything because I reverence and worship God with godly fear. Though others may lack and suffer hunger, I lack none of these things because I seek the Lord by the blood of Jesus and on the authority of His word. No I do not lack any thing that is beneficial for my well-being.

Personal Budget Worksheet

Income				
	Estimated	**Actual**		
Primary Pay				
Other 1				
Other 2				
Total Income				
Expenses				
	Estimated	**Actual**	**Due Date**	**Paid**
Church and Charities				
Tithes				
Offering				
Other Charity 1				
Other Charity 2				
Other Charity 3				
Household Expenses				
Rent/Mortgage				
Electricity				
Gas				
Water				
Grocery				
Household Supplies				
Home Insurance				
Repairs				
Taxes				

Personal Budget Worksheet (continued)

Household Expenses (cont.)				
	Estimated	Actual	Due Date	Paid
Land Phone				
Cable/Dish				
Other				
Car Expenses				
Car Payment				
Car Insurance				
Gas				
Taxes				
Maintenance/Repairs				
Debts				
Creditor 1				
Creditor 2				
Creditor 3				
Creditor 4				
Other				
Medical Expenses				
Medical Insurance				
Life Insurance				
Prescription Med(s)				
Other				

Personal Budget Worksheet (continued)

Other Expenses				
	Estimated	Actual	Due Date	Paid
Savings				
Cell Phone				
Children: Extra-Curricular				
Eateries & Entertainment				
Personal Grooming				
Organization/Club Dues				
Clothing				
Dry Cleaning				
Miscellaneous				
Miscellaneous 1				
Miscellaneous2				
Miscellaneous 3				
Miscellaneous 4				
Total Expenses				

Answers to My Prayers

Mark 11:22-24 And Jesus, replying, said to them, Have faith in God [constantly]. Truly I tell you, whoever says to this mountain, Be lifted up and thrown into the sea! and does not doubt at all in his heart but believes that what he says will take place, it will be done for him. For this reason I am telling you, whatever you ask for in prayer, believe (trust and be confident) that it is granted to you, and you will [get it].

Request	Answer	Date Answered

Request	Answer	Date Answered

Request	Answer	Date Answered

Request	Answer	Date Answered

Challenge!

Where has all the time gone? The year is half spent. You've made great strides. You've journeyed well. You've been blessed to accomplish some if not all of your monthly goals thus far on your war to accomplishing the goals you established for yourself at the beginning of the journey. But not everyone is as blessed as we are. There are many who may be sick, destitute, poor, orphaned, lost and without Christ. Your challenge, should you accept it is share the love of Christ by doing at least one of the following:

1. Take some time to visit, have Bible study, and pray with someone who may be in the hospital.
2. Take some time to visit, have Bible study, and pray with someone who may be in an assisted-living facility.
3. Visit your local soup kitchen and offer your services.
4. Purchase some tracts from your local Christian Book store and share them with people in your community or at the shopping center. Evangelize!
5. If you know of a married couple with children, offer to care for the children for a few hours so that the couple can have some "quality" time together.

Okay. The choice is yours. You have many options, maybe one that's not even on this list. Whatever "challenge" you take, record it below and what the experience meant to you. You may want to encourage a brother or sister to participate in the challenge with you. Be blessed!

_____

_____

Celebration!

Now that you've made preparation to accept your challenge, maybe you've even completed your challenge, it's time to celebrate. Not everyone is willing to give of themselves due to any number of reasons. But not only does God want to bless you, He wants to make YOU a blessing. Look out; the fields around you are ready to be harvested! Sharing God's Love and the gospel can take place in many different ways. Whatever way you chose, I'm proud of you. By all means, take the time to celebrate and record the celebration below.

_____

_____

_____

_____

_____

_____

August

August 2011

Mon	Tues	Wed	Thurs	Fri	Sat	Sun
1	2	3	4	5	6	7
8	9	10	11	12	13	14
15	16	17	18	19	20	21
22	23	24	25	26	27	28
29	30	31				

My Prayer Requests

James 1:5-6a If any of you is deficient in wisdom, let him ask of the giving God [Who gives] to everyone liberally and ungrudgingly, without reproaching or faultfinding, and it will be given him.

Only it must be in faith that he asks with no wavering (no hesitating, no doubting).

Request	Scripture

Request	Scripture

Request	Scripture

Request	Scripture

Monthly Goals

Goal 1 – Spiritual

_____

_____

_____

Goal 2 – Personal

_____

_____

_____

Goal 3 – Financial

_____

_____

_____

Meditations

Week Ending 8-6-2011

Genesis 12:1-4

NOW [in Haran] the Lord said to Abram, Go for yourself [for your own advantage] away from your country, from your relatives and your father's house, to the land that I will show you.

And I will make of you a great nation, and I will bless you [with abundant increase of favors] and make your name famous and distinguished, and you will be a blessing [dispensing good to others].

And I will bless those who bless you [who confer prosperity or happiness upon you] and curse him who curses or uses insolent language toward you; in you will all the families and kindred of the earth be blessed [and by you they will bless themselves].

So Abram departed, as the Lord had directed him; and Lot [his nephew] went with him. Abram was seventy-five years old when he left Haran.

Week Ending 8-13-2011

John 1:1-12

IN THE beginning [before all time] was the Word (Christ), and the Word was with God, and the Word was God Himself.

He was present originally with God.

All things were made and came into existence through Him; and without Him was not even one thing made that has come into being.

In Him was Life, and the Life was the Light of men.

And the Light shines on in the darkness, for the darkness has never overpowered it [put it out or absorbed it or appropriated it, and is unreceptive to it].

There came a man sent from God, whose name was John.

This man came to witness, that he might testify of the Light, that all men might believe in it [adhere to it, trust it, and rely upon it] through him.

He was not the Light himself, but came that he might bear witness regarding the Light.

There it was--the true Light [was then] coming into the world [the genuine, perfect, steadfast Light] that illumines every person.

He came into the world, and though the world was made through Him, the world did not recognize Him [did not know Him].

He came to that which belonged to Him [to His own--His domain, creation, things, world], and they who were His own did not receive Him and did not welcome Him.

But to as many as did receive and welcome Him, He gave the authority (power, privilege, right) to become the children of God, that is, to those who believe in (adhere to, trust in, and rely on) His name--

Week Ending 8-20-2011

The Revelation 4:2-11

At once I came under the [Holy] Spirit's power, and behold, a throne stood in heaven, with One seated on the throne!

And He Who sat there appeared like [the crystalline brightness of] jasper and [the fiery] sardius, and encircling the throne there was a halo that looked like [a rainbow of] emerald.

Twenty-four other thrones surrounded the throne, and seated on these thrones were twenty-four elders (the members of the heavenly Sanhedrin), arrayed in white clothing, with crowns of gold upon their heads.

Out from the throne came flashes of lightning and rumblings and peals of thunder, and in front of the throne seven blazing torches burned, which are the seven Spirits of God [the sevenfold Holy Spirit];

And in front of the throne there was also what looked like a transparent glassy sea, as if of crystal. And around the throne, in the center at each side of the throne, were four living creatures (beings) who were full of eyes in front and behind [with intelligence as to what is before and at the rear of them].

The first living creature (being) was like a lion, the second living creature like an ox, the third living creature had the face of a man, and the fourth living creature [was] like a flying eagle.

And the four living creatures, individually having six wings, were full of eyes all over and within [underneath their wings]; and day and night they never stop saying, Holy, holy, holy is the Lord God Almighty (Omnipotent), Who was and Who is and Who is to come.

And whenever the living creatures offer glory and honor and thanksgiving to Him Who sits on the throne, Who lives forever and ever (through the eternities of the eternities),

The twenty-four elders (the members of the heavenly Sanhedrin) fall prostrate before Him Who is sitting on the throne, and they worship Him Who lives forever and ever; and they throw down their crowns before the throne, crying out,

Worthy are You, our Lord and God, to receive the glory and the honor and dominion, for You created all things; by Your will they were [brought into being] and were created.

Week Ending 8-27-2011

Galatians 2:19-20

For I through the Law [under the operation of the curse of the Law] have [in Christ's death for me] myself died to the Law and all the Law's demands upon me, so that I may [henceforth] live to and for God.

I have been crucified with Christ [in Him I have shared His crucifixion]; it is no longer I who live, but Christ (the Messiah) lives in me; and the life I now live in the body I live by faith in (by adherence to and reliance on and complete trust in) the Son of God, Who loved me and gave Himself up for me.

Monthly Tasks – Appointments

Task	✓
1	
2	
3	
4	
5	
6	
7	
8	

Appointment	Date/Time
1	
2	
3	
4	
5	
6	
7	
8	

Financial Meditation and Confession

Proverbs 8:18-21

Riches and honor are with me, enduring wealth and righteousness (uprightness in every area and relation, and right standing with God).

My fruit is better than gold, yes, than refined gold, and my increase than choice silver.

I [Wisdom] walk in the way of righteousness (moral and spiritual rectitude in every area and relation), in the midst of the paths of justice,

That I may cause those who love me to inherit [true] riches and that I may fill their treasuries.

Confession

I am who the Lord God says I am and I can and will possess what the Lord says I will possess. I walk in the wisdom of God. I choose to follow the path that pleases and honors God. I choose God's way over the way of the world, over the way of man and above my own way. The wisdom of God causes me to walk righteously before Him and before man. Because I have God's wisdom, I also have riches and honor, enduring wealth and righteousness, refined gold and silver. I inherit the fruit of wisdom, true riches, and all my treasuries are full.

Personal Budget Worksheet

Income				
	Estimated	**Actual**		
Primary Pay				
Other 1				
Other 2				
Total Income				
Expenses				
	Estimated	**Actual**	**Due Date**	**Paid**
Church and Charities				
Tithes				
Offering				
Other Charity 1				
Other Charity 2				
Other Charity 3				
Household Expenses				
Rent/Mortgage				
Electricity				
Gas				
Water				
Grocery				
Household Supplies				
Home Insurance				
Repairs				
Taxes				

Personal Budget Worksheet (continued)

Household Expenses (cont.)				
	Estimated	**Actual**	**Due Date**	**Paid**
Land Phone				
Cable/Dish				
Other				
Car Expenses				
Car Payment				
Car Insurance				
Gas				
Taxes				
Maintenance/Repairs				
Debts				
Creditor 1				
Creditor 2				
Creditor 3				
Creditor 4				
Other				
Medical Expenses				
Medical Insurance				
Life Insurance				
Prescription Med(s)				
Other				

Personal Budget Worksheet (continued)

Other Expenses				
	Estimated	Actual	Due Date	Paid
Savings				
Cell Phone				
Children: Extra-Curricular				
Eateries & Entertainment				
Personal Grooming				
Organization/Club Dues				
Clothing				
Dry Cleaning				
Miscellaneous				
Miscellaneous 1				
Miscellaneous2				
Miscellaneous 3				
Miscellaneous 4				
Total Expenses				

Answers to My Prayers

Psalm 34:15 The eyes of the Lord are toward the [uncompromisingly] righteous and His ears are open to their cry.

Request	Scripture

Request	Scripture

Request	Scripture

Request	Scripture

Celebration!

You just keep proving that you can do all things through Christ...He strengthens you! As you continue in the Word of God, truly you are becoming His disciple. God rewards those who will diligently seek Him and I believe that He allows us to reward ourselves. After all, Daddy God is a rewarder, well we should be rewarders too. Take a minute and give a word of "thanks" to someone you admire, someone who has influenced you in a positive way. Let them be a part of your celebration! Whatever you choose to do to celebrate this month's accomplishments, include that individual who has demonstrated the love of God and been that example of righteousness and holiness before you. Take a moment and let them know how much you appreciate them. Record your celebration with the one who inspires you below.

_____

_____

_____

_____

_____

September

September 2011

Mon	Tues	Wed	Thurs	Fri	Sat	Sun
			1	2	3	4
5 Labor Day	6	7	8	9	10	11
12	13	14	15	16	17	18
19	20	21	22	23	24	25
26	27	28	29	30		

My Prayer Requests

II Chronicles 7:14 If My people, who are called by My name, shall humble themselves, pray, seek, crave, and require of necessity My face and turn from their wicked ways, then will I hear from heaven, forgive their sin, and heal their land.

Request	Scripture

Request	Scripture

Request	Scripture

Request	Scripture

Monthly Goals

Goal 1 – Spiritual

_____

_____

_____

Goal 2 – Personal

_____

_____

_____

Goal 3 – Financial

_____

_____

_____

Meditations

Week Ending 9-3-2011

Psalm 37:3-9

Trust (lean on, rely on, and be confident) in the Lord and do good; so shall you dwell in the land and feed surely on His faithfulness, and truly you shall be fed.

Delight yourself also in the Lord, and He will give you the desires and secret petitions of your heart.

Commit your way to the Lord [roll and repose each care of your load on Him]; trust (lean on, rely on, and be confident) also in Him and He will bring it to pass.

And He will make your uprightness and right standing with God go forth as the light, and your justice and right as [the shining sun of] the noonday.

Be still and rest in the Lord; wait for Him and patiently lean yourself upon Him; fret not yourself because of him who prospers in his way, because of the man who brings wicked devices to pass.

Cease from anger and forsake wrath; fret not yourself--it tends only to evildoing.

For evildoers shall be cut off, but those who wait and hope and look for the Lord [in the end] shall inherit the earth.

Week Ending 9-10-2011

Proverbs 6:16-19

These six things the Lord hates, indeed, seven are an abomination to Him:

A proud look [the spirit that makes one overestimate himself and underestimate others], a lying tongue, and hands that shed innocent blood,

A heart that manufactures wicked thoughts and plans, feet that are swift in running to evil,

A false witness who breathes out lies [even under oath], and he who sows discord among his brethren.

Week Ending 9-17-2011

II Timothy 2:19-21

But the firm foundation of (laid by) God stands, sure and unshaken, bearing this seal (inscription): The Lord knows those who are His, and, Let everyone who names [himself by] the name of the Lord give up all iniquity and stand aloof from it.

But in a great house there are not only vessels of gold and silver, but also [utensils] of wood and earthenware, and some for honorable and noble [use] and some for menial and ignoble [use].

So whoever cleanses himself [from what is ignoble and unclean, who separates himself from contact with contaminating and corrupting influences] will [then himself] be a vessel set apart and useful for honorable and noble purposes, consecrated and profitable to the Master, fit and ready for any good work.

Week Ending 9-24-2011

James 1:2-4, 12

Consider it wholly joyful, my brethren, whenever you are enveloped in or encounter trials of any sort or fall into various temptations.

Be assured and understand that the trial and proving of your faith bring out endurance and steadfastness and patience.

But let endurance and steadfastness and patience have full play and do a thorough work, so that you may be [people] perfectly and fully developed [with no defects], lacking in nothing.

Blessed (happy, to be envied) is the man who is patient under trial and stands up under temptation, for when he has stood the test and been approved, he will receive [the victor's] crown of life which God has promised to those who love Him.

Monthly Tasks – Appointments

Task	✓
1	
2	
3	
4	
5	
6	
7	
8	

Appointment	Date/Time
1	
2	
3	
4	
5	
6	
7	
8	

Financial Meditation and Confession

II Corinthians 9:6-11

[Remember] this: he who sows sparingly and grudgingly will also reap sparingly and grudgingly, and he who sows generously [that blessings may come to someone] will also reap generously and with blessings.

Let each one [give] as he has made up his own mind and purposed in his heart, not reluctantly or sorrowfully or under compulsion, for God loves (He takes pleasure in, prizes above other things, and is unwilling to abandon or to do without) a cheerful (joyous, "prompt to do it") giver [whose heart is in his giving].

And God is able to make all grace (every favor and earthly blessing) come to you in abundance, so that you may always and under all circumstances and whatever the need be self-sufficient [possessing enough to require no aid or support and furnished in abundance for every good work and charitable donation].

As it is written, He [the benevolent person] scatters abroad; He gives to the poor; His deeds of justice and goodness and kindness and benevolence will go on and endure forever!

And [God] Who provides seed for the sower and bread for eating will also provide and multiply your [resources for] sowing and increase the fruits of your righteousness [which manifests itself in active goodness, kindness, and charity].

Thus you will be enriched in all things and in every way, so that you can be generous, and [your generosity as it is] administered by us will bring forth thanksgiving to God.

Confession

I am who the Lord God says I am and I can and will possess what the Lord says I will possess. As I sow, I sow generously so that others are generously blessed. And because I sow generously, I reap generously. I have purposed in my heart to give to the work of the Kingdom of God with great joy. I am not slow to give, but I am quick to give. My God takes pleasure in my giving. He makes every favor and earthly blessing come to me in great abundance. I always have more than enough and am furnished in abundance for every good work. I exercise my right as a child of the King to perform deeds of justice, goodness, kindness, and charity and I increase in good deeds. I am enriched in all things, in every way so that I can continue to be generous. I am abounding in goodness, kindness, and acts of charity and good deeds now. I am abounding in the favor and earthly blessing now. The Father takes great pleasure in my giving now.

Personal Budget Worksheet

Income				
	Estimated	**Actual**		
Primary Pay				
Other 1				
Other 2				
Total Income				
Expenses				
	Estimated	**Actual**	**Due Date**	**Paid**
Church and Charities				
Tithes				
Offering				
Other Charity 1				
Other Charity 2				
Other Charity 3				
Household Expenses				
Rent/Mortgage				
Electricity				
Gas				
Water				
Grocery				
Household Supplies				
Home Insurance				
Repairs				
Taxes				

Personal Budget Worksheet (continued)

Household Expenses (cont.)				
	Estimated	Actual	Due Date	Paid
Land Phone				
Cable/Dish				
Other				
Car Expenses				
Car Payment				
Car Insurance				
Gas				
Taxes				
Maintenance/Repairs				
Debts				
Creditor 1				
Creditor 2				
Creditor 3				
Creditor 4				
Other				
Medical Expenses				
Medical Insurance				
Life Insurance				
Prescription Med(s)				
Other				

Personal Budget Worksheet (continued)

Other Expenses				
	Estimated	**Actual**	**Due Date**	**Paid**
Savings				
Cell Phone				
Children: Extra-Curricular				
Eateries & Entertainment				
Personal Grooming				
Organization/Club Dues				
Clothing				
Dry Cleaning				
Miscellaneous				
Miscellaneous 1				
Miscellaneous2				
Miscellaneous 3				
Miscellaneous 4				
Total Expenses				

Answers to My Prayers

Jeremiah 33:3 Call to Me and I will answer you and show you great and mighty things, fenced in and hidden, which you do not know (do not distinguish and recognize, have knowledge of and understand).

Request	Answer	Date Answered

Request	Answer	Date Answered

Request	Answer	Date Answered

Request	Answer	Date Answered

164

Celebration!

Don't let this moment pass you by. You've got it going on. I am bubbling over with joy at the consistency with which you've approached this journey and you should be bubbling over too! Just give yourself a big hug because that's the least you deserve for what you've completed this month. Now that you've hugged yourself, go purchase that item *for yourself* that you've been thinking about. Go ahead. Just do it! You've earned it. But remember do not create any debt or do anything that will put your budget in jeopardy while rewarding yourself. No regrets!

_____

_____

_____

_____

_____

October

October 2011

Mon	Tues	Wed	Thurs	Fri	Sat	Sun
					1	2
3	4	5	6	7	8	9
10	11	12	13	14	15	16
17	18	19	20	21	22	23
24	25	26	27	28	29	30
31						

My Prayer Requests

Romans 8:26 So too the [Holy] Spirit comes to our aid and bears us up in our weakness; for we do not know what prayer to offer nor how to offer it worthily as we ought, but the Spirit Himself goes to meet our supplication and pleads in our behalf with unspeakable yearnings and groanings too deep for utterance.

Request	**Scripture**

Request	**Scripture**

Request	**Scripture**

Request	**Scripture**

Monthly Goals

Goal 1 – Spiritual

_____

_____

_____

Goal 2 – Personal

_____

_____

_____

Goal 3 – Financial

_____

_____

_____

Meditations

Week Ending 10-1-2011

Ephesians 5:15-21

Look carefully then how you walk! Live purposefully and worthily and accurately, not as the unwise and witless, but as wise (sensible, intelligent people),

Making the very most of the time [buying up each opportunity], because the days are evil.

Therefore do not be vague and thoughtless and foolish, but understanding and firmly grasping what the will of the Lord is.

And do not get drunk with wine, for that is debauchery; but ever be filled and stimulated with the [Holy] Spirit.

Speak out to one another in psalms and hymns and spiritual songs, offering praise with voices [and instruments] and making melody with all your heart to the Lord,

At all times and for everything giving thanks in the name of our Lord Jesus Christ to God the Father.

Be subject to one another out of reverence for Christ (the Messiah, the Anointed One).

Week Ending 10-8-2011

Philemon 4-7

I give thanks to my God for you always when I mention you in my prayers,

Because I continue to hear of your love and of your loyal faith which you have toward the Lord Jesus and [which you show] toward all the saints (God's consecrated people).

[And I pray] that the participation in and sharing of your faith may produce and promote full recognition and appreciation and understanding and precise knowledge of every good [thing] that is ours in [our identification with] Christ Jesus [and unto His glory].

For I have derived great joy and comfort and encouragement from your love, because the hearts of the saints [who are your fellow Christians] have been cheered and refreshed through you, [my] brother.

Week Ending 10-15-2011

Zephaniah 3:14-17

Sing, O Daughter of Zion; shout, O Israel! Rejoice, be in high spirits and glory with all your heart, O Daughter of Jerusalem [in that day].

[For then it will be that] the Lord has taken away the judgments against you; He has cast out your enemy. The King of Israel, even the Lord [Himself], is in the midst of you; [and after He has come to you] you shall not experience or fear evil any more.

In that day it shall be said to Jerusalem, Fear not, O Zion. Let not your hands sink down or be slow and listless.

The Lord your God is in the midst of you, a Mighty One, a Savior [Who saves]! He will rejoice over you with joy; He will rest [in silent satisfaction] and in His love He will be silent and make no mention [of past sins, or even recall them]; He will exult over you with singing.

Week Ending 10-22-2011

Hebrews 4:9-12

So then, there is still awaiting a full and complete Sabbath-rest reserved for the [true] people of God;

For he who has once entered [God's] rest also has ceased from [the weariness and pain] of human labors, just as God rested from those labors peculiarly His own.

Let us therefore be zealous and exert ourselves and strive diligently to enter that rest [of God, to know and experience it for ourselves], that no one may fall or perish by the same kind of unbelief and disobedience [into which those in the wilderness fell].

For the Word that God speaks is alive and full of power [making it active, operative, energizing, and effective]; it is sharper than any two-edged sword, penetrating to the dividing line of the breath of life (soul) and [the immortal] spirit, and of joints and marrow [of the deepest parts of our nature], exposing and sifting and analyzing and judging the very thoughts and purposes of the heart.

Week Ending 10-29-2011

Isaiah 41:10

Fear not [there is nothing to fear], for I am with you; do not look around you in terror and be dismayed, for I am your God. I will strengthen and harden you to difficulties, yes, I will help you; yes, I will hold you up and retain you with My [victorious] right hand of rightness and justice.

Monthly Tasks – Appointments

Task	✓
1 _____	_____
2 _____	_____
3 _____	_____
4 _____	_____
5 _____	_____
6 _____	_____
7 _____	_____
8 _____	_____

Appointment	Date/Time
1 _____	_____
2 _____	_____
3 _____	_____
4 _____	_____
5 _____	_____
6 _____	_____
7 _____	_____
8 _____	_____

Financial Meditation and Confession

Deuteronomy 8:1, 6-10, 18

ALL THE commandments which I command you this day you shall be watchful to do, that you may live and multiply and go in and possess the land which the Lord swore to give to your fathers.

So you shall keep the commandments of the Lord your God, to walk in His ways and [reverently] fear Him.

For the Lord your God is bringing you into a good land, a land of brooks of water, of fountains and springs, flowing forth in valleys and hills;

A land of wheat and barley, and vines and fig trees and pomegranates, a land of olive trees and honey;

A land in which you shall eat food without shortage and lack nothing in it; a land whose stones are iron and out of whose hills you can dig copper.

When you have eaten and are full, then you shall bless the Lord your God for all the good land which He has given you.

But you shall [earnestly] remember the Lord your God, for it is He Who gives you power to get wealth, that He may establish His covenant which He swore to your fathers, as it is this day.

Confession

I am who the Lord God says I am and I can and will possess what the Lord says I will possess. My God has established His covenant with me and because I walk in obedience to His Word, He causes me to take possession of the land promised to Abraham and to his seed. I keep the commandments of the Lord. He brings me into a good land, a land that is rich, a land in which there is no scarceness and I will not lack anything in that land. I bless the Lord. He causes me to eat and I am full. I remember that it is not by my power, might, or ability, but it is the Lord who has done this great thing in my life. He continually gives me the power to obtain wealth that His covenant with His people may be established.

Personal Budget Worksheet

Income				
	Estimated	**Actual**		
Primary Pay				
Other 1				
Other 2				
Total Income				
Expenses				
	Estimated	**Actual**	**Due Date**	**Paid**
Church and Charities				
Tithes				
Offering				
Other Charity 1				
Other Charity 2				
Other Charity 3				
Household Expenses				
Rent/Mortgage				
Electricity				
Gas				
Water				
Grocery				
Household Supplies				
Home Insurance				
Repairs				
Taxes				

Personal Budget Worksheet (continued)

Household Expenses (cont.)				
	Estimated	**Actual**	**Due Date**	**Paid**
Land Phone				
Cable/Dish				
Other				
Car Expenses				
Car Payment				
Car Insurance				
Gas				
Taxes				
Maintenance/Repairs				
Debts				
Creditor 1				
Creditor 2				
Creditor 3				
Creditor 4				
Other				
Medical Expenses				
Medical Insurance				
Life Insurance				
Prescription Med(s)				
Other				

Personal Budget Worksheet (continued)

Other Expenses				
	Estimated	Actual	Due Date	Paid
Savings				
Cell Phone				
Children: Extra-Curricular				
Eateries & Entertainment				
Personal Grooming				
Organization/Club Dues				
Clothing				
Dry Cleaning				
Miscellaneous				
Miscellaneous 1				
Miscellaneous2				
Miscellaneous 3				
Miscellaneous 4				
Total Expenses				

Answers to My Prayers

Job 42:10 And the Lord turned the captivity of Job and restored his fortunes, when he prayed for his friends; also the Lord gave Job twice as much as he had before.

Request	Answer	Date Answered

Request	Answer	Date Answered

Request	Answer	Date Answered

Request	Answer	Date Answered

Celebration!

Pamper yourself. I'm sure that you spend lots of time seeing to the needs of others, but today is your day. Start by looking in the mirror and repeating after me: "I am fearfully and wonderfully made. I am made in the image of God. I am His creation. I am His and He is mine. I am healed. I am delivered. I am set free. I am strong in the Lord and in the power of His might. Today is a great day for I serve a great God who is with me all the time." Okay...looking good. Make this a "spa" day – just relax. What makes you happy? What gives you pleasure? What is it that calms you? That is what I encourage you to do. Peace!

_____

_____

_____

_____

_____

November

November 2011

Mon	Tues	Wed	Thurs	Fri	Sat	Sun
	1	2	3	4	5	6
7	8	9	10	11	12	13
14	15	16	17	18	19	20
21	22	23	24 Thanksgiving Day	25	26	27
28	29	30				

My Prayer Requests

II Chronicles 6:19 Have respect therefore to the prayer of thy servant, and to his supplication, O LORD my God, to hearken unto the cry and the prayer which thy servant prayeth before thee.

Request	Scripture

Request	Scripture

Request	Scripture

Request	Scripture

Monthly Goals

Goal 1 – Spiritual

_____

_____

_____

Goal 2 – Personal

_____

_____

_____

Goal 3 – Financial

_____

_____

_____

Meditations

Week Ending 11-5-2011

Psalm 119:9-16

How shall a young man cleanse his way? By taking heed and keeping watch [on himself] according to Your word [conforming his life to it].

With my whole heart have I sought You, inquiring for and of You and yearning for You; Oh, let me not wander or step aside [either in ignorance or willfully] from Your commandments.

Your word have I laid up in my heart, that I might not sin against You.

Blessed are You, O Lord; teach me Your statutes.

With my lips have I declared and recounted all the ordinances of Your mouth.

I have rejoiced in the way of Your testimonies as much as in all riches.

I will meditate on Your precepts and have respect to Your ways [the paths of life marked out by Your law].

I will delight myself in Your statutes; I will not forget Your word.

Week Ending 11-12-2011

Ecclesiastes 5:1-7

KEEP YOUR foot [give your mind to what you are doing] when you go [as Jacob to sacred Bethel] to the house of God. For to draw near to hear and obey is better than to give the sacrifice of fools [carelessly, irreverently] too ignorant to know that they are doing evil.

Be not rash with your mouth, and let not your heart be hasty to utter a word before God. For God is in heaven, and you are on earth; therefore let your words be few.

For a dream comes with much business and painful effort, and a fool's voice with many words.

When you vow a vow or make a pledge to God, do not put off paying it; for God has no pleasure in fools (those who witlessly mock Him). Pay what you vow.

It is better that you should not vow than that you should vow and not pay.

Do not allow your mouth to cause your body to sin, and do not say before the messenger [the priest] that it was an error or mistake. Why should God be [made] angry at your voice and destroy the work of your hands?

For in a multitude of dreams there is futility and worthlessness, and ruin in a flood of words. But [reverently] fear God [revere and worship Him, knowing that He is].

Week Ending 11-19-2011

Acts 2:43-47

And a sense of awe (reverential fear) came upon every soul, and many wonders and signs were performed through the apostles (the special messengers).

And all who believed (who adhered to and trusted in and relied on Jesus Christ) were united and [together] they had everything in common;

And they sold their possessions (both their landed property and their movable goods) and distributed the price among all, according as any had need.

And day after day they regularly assembled in the temple with united purpose, and in their homes they broke bread [including the Lord's Supper]. They partook of their food with gladness and simplicity and generous hearts,

Constantly praising God and being in favor and goodwill with all the people; and the Lord kept adding [to their number] daily those who were being saved [from spiritual death].

Week Ending 11-26-2011

Isaiah 26:2-4

Open the gates, that the [uncompromisingly] righteous nation which keeps her faith and her troth [with God] may enter in.

You will guard him and keep him in perfect and constant peace whose mind [both its inclination and its character] is stayed on You, because he commits himself to You, leans on You, and hopes confidently in You.

So trust in the Lord (commit yourself to Him, lean on Him, hope confidently in Him) forever; for the Lord God is an everlasting Rock [the Rock of Ages].

Monthly Tasks – Appointments

Task	✔
1	
2	
3	
4	
5	
6	
7	
8	

Appointment	Date/Time
1	
2	
3	
4	
5	
6	
7	
8	

Financial Meditation and Confession

Proverbs 13:22

A good man leaves an inheritance [of moral stability and goodness] to his children's children, and the wealth of the sinner [finds its way eventually] into the hands of the righteous, for whom it was laid up.

Confession

I am who the Lord God says I am and I can and will possess what the Lord says I will possess. I am a good man and I leave an inheritance of moral stability and goodness to my children's children. The wealth of the sinner, the silver and the gold, the diamonds and the rubies, the houses and the land, is no longer laid up, but it finds its' way into my hands now, for I am the righteousness of God in Christ Jesus and the rightful owner. This wealth is no longer laid up or stored away. But I take possession of it, even today in Jesus' name. I am blessed. My children are blessed. My children's children are blessed because we choose to walk in the finished work of our Lord and Savior Jesus the Christ. I am wealthy.

Personal Budget Worksheet

Income				
	Estimated	**Actual**		
Primary Pay				
Other 1				
Other 2				
Total Income				
Expenses				
	Estimated	**Actual**	**Due Date**	**Paid**
Church and Charities				
Tithes				
Offering				
Other Charity 1				
Other Charity 2				
Other Charity 3				
Household Expenses				
Rent/Mortgage				
Electricity				
Gas				
Water				
Grocery				
Household Supplies				
Home Insurance				
Repairs				
Taxes				

Personal Budget Worksheet (continued)

Household Expenses (cont.)				
	Estimated	Actual	Due Date	Paid
Land Phone				
Cable/Dish				
Other				
Car Expenses				
Car Payment				
Car Insurance				
Gas				
Taxes				
Maintenance/Repairs				
Debts				
Creditor 1				
Creditor 2				
Creditor 3				
Creditor 4				
Other				
Medical Expenses				
Medical Insurance				
Life Insurance				
Prescription Med(s)				
Other				

Personal Budget Worksheet (continued)

Other Expenses				
	Estimated	Actual	Due Date	Paid
Savings				
Cell Phone				
Children: Extra-Curricular				
Eateries & Entertainment				
Personal Grooming				
Organization/Club Dues				
Clothing				
Dry Cleaning				
Miscellaneous				
Miscellaneous 1				
Miscellaneous2				
Miscellaneous 3				
Miscellaneous 4				
Total Expenses				

Answers to My Prayers

Psalm 20:6 Now I know that the Lord saves His anointed; He will answer him from His holy heaven with the saving strength of His right hand.

Request	Answer	Date Answered

Request	Answer	Date Answered

Request	Answer	Date Answered

Request	Answer	Date Answered

Celebration!

WOW! You've been on this journey now for 11 months. What a major accomplishment. You are walking into your destiny, one day at a time, one month at a time and I know it must feel good. You are a living testimony. Now what do you plan to do to celebrate yourself and the strides that you've made on this journey? The choice is yours. Record your celebration below!

_____

_____

_____

_____

_____

_____

December

December 2011

Mon	Tues	Wed	Thurs	Fri	Sat	Sun
			1	2	3	4
5	6	7	8	9	10	11
12	13	14	15	16	17	18
19	20	21	22	23	24	25 Christmas Day
26	27	28	29	30	31 New Year's Eve	

My Prayer Requests

Psalm 5:2-3 Hearken unto the voice of my cry, my King, and my God: for unto thee will I pray.

My voice shalt thou hear in the morning, O LORD; in the morning will I direct my prayer unto thee, and will look up.

Request	**Scripture**

Request	**Scripture**

Request	**Scripture**

Request	**Scripture**

Monthly Goals

Goal 1 – Spiritual

_____

_____

_____

Goal 2 – Personal

_____

_____

_____

Goal 3 – Financial

_____

_____

_____

Meditations

Week Ending 12-3-2011

Romans 13:7-10, 13-14

Render to all men their dues. [Pay] taxes to whom taxes are due, revenue to whom revenue is due, respect to whom respect is due, and honor to whom honor is due.

Keep out of debt and owe no man anything, except to love one another; for he who loves his neighbor [who practices loving others] has fulfilled the Law [relating to one's fellowmen, meeting all its requirements].

The commandments, You shall not commit adultery, You shall not kill, You shall not steal, You shall not covet (have an evil desire), and any other commandment, are summed up in the single command, You shall love your neighbor as [you do] yourself.

Love does no wrong to one's neighbor [it never hurts anybody]. Therefore love meets all the requirements and is the fulfilling of the Law.

Let us live and conduct ourselves honorably and becomingly as in the [open light of] day, not in reveling (carousing) and drunkenness, not in immorality and debauchery (sensuality and licentiousness), not in quarreling and jealousy.

But clothe yourself with the Lord Jesus Christ (the Messiah), and make no provision for [indulging] the flesh [put a stop to thinking about the evil cravings of your physical nature] to [gratify its] desires (lusts).

Week Ending 12-10-2011

I Corinthians 13:4-8, 13

Love endures long and is patient and kind; love never is envious nor boils over with jealousy, is not boastful or vainglorious, does not display itself haughtily.

It is not conceited (arrogant and inflated with pride); it is not rude (unmannerly) and does not act unbecomingly. Love (God's love in us) does not insist on its own rights or its own way, for it is not self-seeking; it is not touchy or fretful or resentful; it takes no account of the evil done to it [it pays no attention to a suffered wrong].

It does not rejoice at injustice and unrighteousness, but rejoices when right and truth prevail.

Love bears up under anything and everything that comes, is ever ready to believe the best of every person, its hopes are fadeless under all circumstances, and it endures everything [without weakening].

Love never fails [never fades out or becomes obsolete or comes to an end]. As for prophecy (the gift of interpreting the divine will and purpose), it will be fulfilled and pass away; as for tongues, they will be destroyed and cease; as for knowledge, it will pass away [it will lose its value and be superseded by truth].

And so faith, hope, love abide [faith--conviction and belief respecting man's relation to God and divine things; hope--joyful and confident expectation of eternal salvation; love--true affection for God and man, growing out of God's love for and in us], these three; but the greatest of these is love.

Week Ending 12-17-2011

I Chronicles 4:10

Jabez cried to the God of Israel, saying, Oh, that You would bless me and enlarge my border, and that Your hand might be with me, and You would keep me from evil so it might not hurt me! And God granted his request.

Week Ending 12-24-2011

Luke 1:26-33

Now in the sixth month [after that], the angel Gabriel was sent from God to a town of Galilee named Nazareth,

To a girl never having been married and a virgin engaged to be married to a man whose name was Joseph, a descendant of the house of David; and the virgin's name was Mary.

And he came to her and said, Hail, O favored one [endued with grace]! The Lord is with you! Blessed (favored of God) are you before all other women!

But when she saw him, she was greatly troubled and disturbed and confused at what he said and kept revolving in her mind what such a greeting might mean.

And the angel said to her, Do not be afraid, Mary, for you have found grace (free, spontaneous, absolute favor and loving-kindness) with God.

And listen! You will become pregnant and will give birth to a Son, and you shall call His name Jesus.

He will be great (eminent) and will be called the Son of the Most High; and the Lord God will give to Him the throne of His forefather David,

And He will reign over the house of Jacob throughout the ages; and of His reign there will be no end.

Week Ending 12-31-2011

Isaiah 42:8-9

I am the Lord; that is My name! And My glory I will not give to another, nor My praise to graven images.

Behold, the former things have come to pass, and new things I now declare; before they spring forth I tell you of them.

Isaiah 43:18-19

Do not [earnestly] remember the former things; neither consider the things of old.

Behold, I am doing a new thing! Now it springs forth; do you not perceive and know it and will you not give heed to it? I will even make a way in the wilderness and rivers in the desert.

Monthly Tasks – Appointments

Task	✔
1	
2	
3	
4	
5	
6	
7	
8	

Appointment	Date/Time
1	
2	
3	
4	
5	
6	
7	
8	

Financial Meditation and Confession

III John 1:2

Beloved, I pray that you may prosper in every way and [that your body] may keep well, even as [I know] your soul keeps well and prospers.

Confession

I am who the Lord God says I am and I can and will possess what the Lord says I will possess. Through time in the Word of God, prayer and fellowship with God the Father, God the Son, and God the Holy Spirit, as well as the body of Christ, my soul prospers. And because my soul prospers in the Word of God, I prosper in my Spirit, in my Body, and in every area of my life. I am in good health. My mind is well. My body is well. My spirit is well. Not only do I prosper spiritually, but I prosper financially. This is the will of God for me and for my family.

Personal Budget Worksheet

Income				
	Estimated	**Actual**		
Primary Pay				
Other 1				
Other 2				
Total Income				
Expenses				
	Estimated	**Actual**	**Due Date**	**Paid**
Church and Charities				
Tithes				
Offering				
Other Charity 1				
Other Charity 2				
Other Charity 3				
Household Expenses				
Rent/Mortgage				
Electricity				
Gas				
Water				
Grocery				
Household Supplies				
Home Insurance				
Repairs				
Taxes				

Personal Budget Worksheet (continued)

Household Expenses (cont.)				
	Estimated	Actual	Due Date	Paid
Land Phone				
Cable/Dish				
Other				
Car Expenses				
Car Payment				
Car Insurance				
Gas				
Taxes				
Maintenance/Repairs				
Debts				
Creditor 1				
Creditor 2				
Creditor 3				
Creditor 4				
Other				
Medical Expenses				
Medical Insurance				
Life Insurance				
Prescription Med(s)				
Other				

Personal Budget Worksheet (continued)

Other Expenses				
	Estimated	Actual	Due Date	Paid
Savings				
Cell Phone				
Children: Extra-Curricular				
Eateries & Entertainment				
Personal Grooming				
Organization/Club Dues				
Clothing				
Dry Cleaning				
Miscellaneous				
Miscellaneous 1				
Miscellaneous2				
Miscellaneous 3				
Miscellaneous 4				
Total Expenses				

Answers to My Prayers

II Corinthians 1:20 For as many as are the promises of God, they all find their Yes [answer] in Him [Christ]. For this reason we also utter the Amen (so be it) to God through Him [in His Person and by His agency] to the glory of God.

Request	Answer	Date Answered

Request	Answer	Date Answered

Request	Answer	Date Answered

Request	Answer	Date Answered

My 2011 Spiritual, Personal, and Financial Accomplishments

Spiritual:

_____

_____

_____

_____

Personal:

_____

_____

_____

_____

Financial:

_____

_____

_____

_____

Celebration!

---

12 months! Congratulations. I hope you can hear the bells and whistles and see the fireworks in celebration of your accomplishment. You've finished what you started! Maybe every goal wasn't met. It's possible that not every task was achieved. But if you can think of just one thing ... that one thing is worth celebrating. You have proven over and over and over again that all things are possible if you just believe. I have believed in you and you have believed in yourself. But most of all, before the very foundation of the world, God believed in you! This should be your biggest celebration yet! Go on...do something that is absolutely extraordinary. You deserve it and so much more!

_____

_____

_____

_____

_____

_____

You've come to the end of this journey....

2011. This is the year that you chose to take the journey of a lifetime. This is the year that you chose a different path and because you chose this path, your life is different. Don't believe what the enemy will speak to your mind...You **have** grown. You've done things that you probably otherwise would not have done. You set goals. You defined tasks. You did a budget...yes you! You've spent much time in prayer and you've seen your prayers answered. Your spirit is more attuned to God because of the time you spent fellowshipping with God the Father, God the Son, and God the Holy Spirit. You've encouraged others through the testimony you've given. You have achieved a measure of "good" success simply because you made decisions and choices that were based on the Word of God. What faith! You held on and refused to let go. I'm sure you were tempted, but you remained faithful to the commitment that you made. Hallelujah! You rose above the temptation to quit, give up, even to turn around and throw in the towel. You persevered. You pressed toward the mark of the high calling of God in Christ Jesus! As you have transitioned in thought and speech through meditation of God's Word and the doing of that Word, you have positioned yourself for the blessings of God to run after you and overtake you. Expect increase! Expect harvest! The seed of the Word of God has been planted in your heart. You have been eternally changed and nothing can ever take that away from you! Thank you for allowing me to share this journey with you.

Maybe, just maybe, you'll **BEGIN A NEW/CONTINUE THE JOURNEY** in 2012...Peace!

Contact & Booking Information:
Rev. Billie D. Hanes
c/o The Greater Canaan Missionary Baptist Church
1764-E Hwy 119N
P.O. Box 21
Mebane, NC 27302
(919) 563-2837
billiehanes@yahoo.com